Strategies to Support Children Autism and Other Complex N

Working with young children on the autistic spectrum and supporting them as they learn can be fascinating, challenging, often overwhelmingly difficult, but more than anything else, hugely rewarding.

Strategies to Support Children with Autism and Other Complex Needs bridges the gap between explaining what autism is and finding ways to interact through having a balance of play activities interspersed with more formal teaching of skills of everyday living. This highly practical text provides a bank of strategies that are specially designed to be matched to the developmental status of each child. These strategies are endorsed by academics who have monitored the children's responses in communicating, pretending, playing, moving and singing, and describe how the children have responded positively over time.

This book covers a variety of topics such as:

- the importance of play for enhancing learning for children with autism and other complex needs;
- evaluating different ways of developing communication;
- transferring learning from one environment to another to aid memorizing;
- understanding the impact of sensory hypo and hyperactivity on children's learning;
- developing a 'Theory of Mind';
- the importance of movement, music and having fun.

Observation and assessment schedules are provided, along with clear and helpful evaluation forms which show staff in primary and early years settings how children on the autistic spectrum can be helped to make meaningful and encouraging progress.

This text is a vital read for any practitioners working with children on the autistic spectrum or with complex learning difficulties.

Christine Macintyre was formerly a senior lecturer in Child Development, Play and Special Needs at the University of Edinburgh, UK. She now works as an early education consultant.

Strategies to Support Children with Autism and Other Complex Needs

Resources for teachers, support staff and parents

Christine Macintyre

Routledge
Taylor & Francis Group

LONDON AND NEW YORK

First published 2016
by Routledge
2 Park Square, Milton Park, Abingdon, Oxon OX14 4RN

and by Routledge
711 Third Avenue, New York, NY 10017

Routledge is an imprint of the Taylor & Francis Group, an informa business

© 2016 C. Macintyre

British Library Cataloguing in Publication Data
A catalogue record for this book is available from the British Library

Library of Congress Cataloging-in-Publication Data
Macintyre, Christine, 1938–
    Strategies to support children with autism and other complex needs: resources for teachers, support staff and parents / Christine Macintyre.
        pages cm
    1. Autistic children—Education. 2. Autism in children. I. Title.
    LC4717.M317 2016
    371.94—dc23   2015017263

ISBN: 978-1-138-91892-4 (hbk)
ISBN: 978-1-138-91893-1 (pbk)
ISBN: 978-1-315-68816-9 (ebk)

Typeset in Sabon
by Keystroke, Station Road, Codsall, Wolverhampton
Printed and bound in Great Britain by
Ashford Colour Press Ltd, Gosport, Hampshire

Contents

Acknowledgements

There were many people who made this book possible and my heartfelt thanks go to them all.

First of all, so many thanks to the children's parents, the headteacher, Mrs Kirsty Rosie, and all her staff who allowed me to be in school to see and understand the practice that built such a happy and productive learning environment for children with different learning differences. Many of these children have an autistic spectrum condition and others have complex conditions such as ADHD (attention deficit hyperactivity disorder), Fragile X and Down's syndrome. The positive atmosphere in every class sparked the motivation for this book that asked the professionals to share the strategies they had devised to support their children and helped them learn in a happy, stress-free way.

The children themselves set the group of professionals (later called the team) challenges in deciding what was best for each one and in responding or indeed in leading play developments; they provided joy and fun and sadness just as all children do. The team carefully monitored their development and selected the most appropriate strategies to enhance their learning. The ideas were researched in journals and books a) to ensure that they could all be justified in academic ways b) to find if new writings could suggest additional or alternative strategies c) to find what benefits could realistically be expected and d) to provide a resource for future study and ongoing action and research. There is also an extensive bibliography to provide additional information that is outwith the scope of this book.

The children's parents wholeheartedly supported the investigation. They were generous in giving permission for the team to compile case studies of their children so that readers could get to know them in their learning environment. In this way we hoped that readers could empathise with the children and recognise how the strategies found to be successful in this venue could be adopted or amended for use in their own setting or at home.

As in all books, the children's names are changed and in photographs some of their faces are blurred, but the text describes real events with real children. I do hope the joy does not disappear with the blurring! What is hidden is the expressiveness of the eyes and the smiles especially when the children learn to communicate. This is especially revealing in non-verbal children but there are other, possibly social reasons why faces cannot be shown. The wishes of the parents have been respected at all times. The photographs are very important as they illustrate the progress the children make as the strategies are put into action. They show the pleasure the children gain and the resources that stimulate them to learn through play.

The parents also provided information about the children's wellbeing at home in the daily diaries which passed from home to school and they were regularly welcomed as visitors into school. These measures allowed both parents and staff to communicate successes and concerns (e.g. on occasion, if the team found it difficult to tell if certain children were happy, the parents would confirm that they were eager to come to school or perhaps explain some home incident that might have concerned the child). And so when successes or worries occurred they could be immediately shared and ways to move forward could be developed together in the sure understanding that everyone was doing their best to support the child.

Throughout the study, the cooperation of the professionals in school was so important. They all had different specialist interests and levels of experience. What they had in common was total commitment to the children and a real belief that they would all blossom! The headteacher and other senior staff supported the work too. They were constantly contributing ideas and providing more resources so that different strategies could be tried. The caterpillar for the garden was specially bought to encourage crawling although Leon discovered a new balance challenge!

Very patient teachers, nursery nurses and teaching support staff shared their observations, their plans and their strategies; physical education specialists and occupational therapists planned together developing ideas and reflecting on their practice with many smiles, sometimes sadness and always asking questions as to why some things worked while others stalled. In this positive atmosphere everyone gained a deeper understanding of how to optimise the children's learning. Music, speech, art and occupational therapists made significant contributions too, thus making education for the children rich in every sphere. The four aspects of development, i.e. intellectual, motor, social and emotional, provided a base for planning and assessing thus ensuring that a balanced curriculum was part of each day.

All the team hoped that the increased workload they had to fulfil the demands of the study would provide new insights that could be used to build the most appropriate and stimulating learning strategies for many of the children who had complex needs. The team worked together to find play activities to engage children in their learning, to foster pretending and so develop a theory of mind. And through gaining self-esteem, the team hoped that the children would become more competent in carrying out the activities of daily living, for after all 'it is to the young that the future belongs'.

Many thanks to the professional team at Keystroke for the lovely organisation of the text. Thank you too to the team at Routledge for the professional presentation of the text. Different contributors led by Senior Publisher Alison Foyle and Senior Editorial Assistant Sarah Tuckwell are unfailingly cheerful and helpful. I have written many books for them and their support has been constant and stimulating. My grateful thanks goes to them all.

Preamble

This text explains a project that invited experienced professionals who taught children with complex needs, (primarily autistic spectrum conditions) to share their expertise with others. The aim in so doing is to find whether a bank of tried and tested strategies in one venue could ease the learning path for pupils and teachers in another so that they might enjoy and more fully benefit from their time in school. (The change in terminology from autistic spectrum disorder to autistic spectrum condition is a new but more gentle description. The change is similar to the move from learning difficulties to learning differences. These changes remove any sense of 'blame' or negativity.)

The team were first asked to share observations of their children through compiling brief but personal case studies. The next step was to explain and justify the strategies they devised to support the children's learning and in evaluating them (for ideas didn't always work first time), endorse or amend their choice. This was so that readers could appreciate the responses of the children in their learning context and so judge whether the suggested strategies could be helpful in their own setting.

Today, the National Autistic Society (NAS) explains that the number of people in the UK affected by autism has risen to 700,000 (adults and children) and more children are affected by Fragile X, Down's syndrome and global developmental delay too. The policy of inclusion means that many children with these and other complex needs are in mainstream settings and sometimes the professionals there have not had the opportunity to interact with and teach children who learn differently. Finding how each individual child learns best is challenging especially if the children are non-verbal. Sadly, throughout the UK, parents of 40 per cent of children report that they are not happy with the schools their children attend (NAS 2015) because the class numbers and the ever changing routines are not ideal for children with these conditions. It is hoped that the strategies explained in this book will provide support, even inspiration, so that more professionals will enjoy teaching these lovely children. And if the strategies are not immediately transferable to different situations, possibly because of the different context and the numbers of children to be taught, it is hoped that they can be readily amended.

Alongside the strategies, there are a range of theoretical explanations that explain the implications of having complex needs and show some of the detailed research that is being done. These demonstrate that the choice of each strategy is not 'ad hoc' but has been carefully considered and justified in recent academic writings and in knowledge of each child's needs. This is really a 'dip in' book that allows readers to follow different children and understand how they became more confident and competent, i.e. how they blossomed over time.

General strategies

Just before setting out and as this book is all about strategies that give ideas for interaction, the team compiled a list of general strategies or pieces of advice that they would share with new members of staff. These were:

- Enjoy the children. Get to know each child beyond any 'label' they have been given. They are children with a difficulty that is not their fault – not difficult children. Find how they learn best and adapt plans to suit their preferred way.
- Smile a lot and always be patient – our children often need extra time to build up trust. The aim is to have an oasis of calm so that the children can approach you confidently.
- Build a routine, e.g. sing the same songs to signify regrouping in the teaching circle. These let the children recognise when it is time to change activities and gives them time to respond. Routine gives our children security.
- Don't rush in. Stay back and give the children time to get to know you. For many children 'the world goes too fast'. Use the first days to learn each child's name and build up positive observations about the things each child can do.
- Recognise that, while developing eye contact is very important, too much too soon can overwhelm some children and cause them to withdraw. Similarly 'over enthusiasm' can confuse children who need calm. Remember that sensory over-load is a common trait.
- Let the children play and try to follow their lead. Give them plenty of time to play if they are happy to do so. Notice what they play at, if they watch others and copy or learn to pretend. Monitor if and when they choose to communicate with others and how they do so. Perhaps call this play time, 'Golden Time' so that the children know this is a critically important part of the learning timetable.
- Keep language to a minimum in the early days. Use key words and gentle gestures to convey support.
- Slow down and speak clearly – the children need time to process what they see and hear.
- Let the children see you respect them, their families and their home environment. This is done by sending home positive notes – the parents are desperate to hear good news – and letting the parents know you are grateful for their input in helping their child at school.
- Show you empathise with families who find it difficult to cope. Some families have more than one child with special needs. They may need extra provisions

such as nappies or special dietary shopping. This all takes time and money and is a 24/7 commitment.

- Be positive. 'Catch the children being good' and praise them immediately to boost their self-esteem. If they do not enjoy overt praise, a smile or a tap on the shoulder or a sticker will convey that you are pleased. When something very good happens, let the child choose the 'reward', for something you choose may not be favoured!
- Focus on achievement while paying attention to other aspects. Avoid always seeing 'support' as dealing with difficulties. Following the children's lead will convey the message that you value what they choose to do.
- Try to ignore minor upsets to prevent the same child's name always being called out.
- If a child becomes fractious, divert the other children till calm is restored.
- See the learning environment through the children's eyes and reduce noise, light and 'traffic' whenever possible. Simple changes can engender calm. Careful organisation can settle the children.
- Arrange the furniture so that there are no open runways especially if there are children who love to charge around. Make a safe runway outside.
- Small spaces can help security. Reduce the space, e.g. in the gym, till the children feel secure.
- The learning environment should always respond to sensory difficulties. Children with impaired hearing have to be near the teacher and away from any source of noise distraction e.g. a radiator that fizzes, even earrings that jangle. Children with visual difficulties should have shielded lights and be able to move out of direct sunlight. Those who find it difficult to stay still can be calmed by sitting on a beanbag that allows a modicum of movement. Many children have to move to feel balanced and secure. A beanbag allows this.
- Many children can 'listen better' if they have something to hold or stroke. If all their proprioceptors are working their sensory input is enhanced.
- Allow 'chill out time' so that if any children feel tense or over stimulated they can be private for a short time. A walk round the school with a trusted buddy can alleviate anxiety and help focus. Alternatively a child may wish to be in a safe space 'alone' or with a toy for a short spell.
- Allow the children to use headphones that give a calming, white noise. This helps reduce distractors from the environment and encourages focus. These can also reduce over-sensitive hearing.
- In class have a visual timetable so that the children can see what comes next. In the beginning remove the pictures when the learning episode is over to help the children understand the sequence of the day, but once this is understood arrange the episodes as a clock with a pointing hand that moves around. This conveys the passing of time. An opportunity to transfer learning from this to recognising numbers on a clock might be possible.
- Visual timetables are very important – for examples see Appendix 2. These save remembering, relieve anxiety and promote independence! The same ones can be used at home and in school. These are particularly useful for sharing planning and sequencing activities with the children. Sometimes children can do the discrete parts of a task but can't plan or appreciate what comes first, then next.

- Let the children know of any change in their routine in plenty of time. 'Unexpected treats' are often not so! They may cause alarm and upset.
- If children are unexpectedly aggressive or withdrawn, remember something at home may have distressed them and they may need time and calm to refocus.
- Become part of a team with *all* the support staff. All staff are there to support and encourage the children and they all have experiences to share. Sometimes 'helpers on the school bus' or kitchen staff can be the first to suspect a child is unwell.
- For children in the mainstream classroom: let children choose where they wish to sit – they are often more at ease at the back of the room so that there are no 'surprises' e.g. jolts or someone encroaching on their personal space behind them. Similarly when the children line up to leave the classroom, the children may prefer to be at the back so that they can follow the others.
- Give the children as much advance notice of personnel or curriculum changes as possible – avoid 'surprises'.
- Work with the children's strengths e.g. if they are good at maths, can mathematical experiences be highlighted in other lessons e.g. being in charge of the till in the 'shop' or being responsible for making and counting tickets for the school bus or if they like music can they be in charge of a tape recorder and have their choice of music in class?
- Enjoy the children and their successes – they will happen. Don't panic, ask for help.

Good luck!

Introduction
Setting the scene

Supporting children with learning differences or difficulties, autism and other complex needs is at once a tremendous pleasure and a significant challenge. This is because each of the children is intriguingly different; each one has an individual profile of abilities and often subtle needs. So teaching them requires much more than a detailed academic knowledge of their 'condition' even if they have a sure diagnosis; it needs understanding of each child's particular strengths and difficulties, patience and a very special empathy. This is because many of the children will not have the instinctive understandings to anticipate or to participate in the usual learning activities or speech to make their wishes known. To flourish they need a calm, supportive routine and very often 1:1 support.

Despite their learning differences, however, most children will be happy and content in school, especially when they recognise how well they are nurtured there and they will gradually respond to a routine that is predictable and safe with staff that understand and respect them. Some children will take longer to settle; some may remain withdrawn and anxious for a considerable time; in the earliest days they might even resist attempts to help them. Perhaps this is because they do not yet understand the world of the classroom and the children and adults who work there and, lacking speech, they cannot explain what they would like to do. They may not be able to communicate how they are feeling or have the social or emotional nous to know how to make a friend. They may have sensory difficulties that make being in a busy classroom overwhelmingly difficult; they may be confused by moving from home to a very different environment. Without verbal communication, how can they explain that they are distressed by the changing routines of the day, by noises outside, by flickering lights, by the intrusion of a stranger into the class or even that a planned teaching episode has interrupted their play? How can they communicate the pleasure repeating activities or lining up bricks gives, when to neurotypical children and adults these activities might appear meaningless or sad?

Practitioners have to develop understandings of the children's perspective on their world. Through careful observations they have to gauge what is giving satisfaction or causing upset, then judge the kind and timing of interventions that are appropriate. They often have to try a range of different strategies to find a way to interest or to placate the children while at the same time designing ways to achieve curriculum goals. This is not an easy thing to do.

Alternatively, practitioners, knowing their children and keyed in to how they are thinking and developing, may decide to stay back and keep observing and recording in order to leave the ownership of a play activity with the child. This is not laissez-faire; this is a reasoned choice based on experience and knowledge about the children and what they are doing and learning. Children can easily be overwhelmed by asking them to do too much too soon.

Decisions about the kind and the timing of intervention are particularly difficult to make especially during play when the staff follow the children's lead, aiming to understand what they are doing and feeling as a basis for subtly extending their skills. But the benefits of a play-based curriculum, e.g. that the children learn in a stress-free environment and gain the confidence to push back boundaries in each aspect of development, outweigh the complexities of observation and planning. There is also evidence that the symbolic play of children with autistic spectrum conditions (ASCs) can highlight language potentials. Lewis (2003) regards play as instrumental in developing both the comprehension and production of language. She claims that as they play children learn strategies for solving problems; they link names with objects and begin to form event schemas.

With all this inherent potential, the timing of any intervention is crucial. How can professionals tell when something significant might be about to happen? With time constraints and other children to support, it can be difficult for staff to 'wait and see', i.e. to find out if the children will develop an idea that could herald a real breakthrough. Yet staff know that hasty and possibly inappropriate or over-ambitious interventions can cut any learning right down.

Difficult decisions like this come from knowing the children, and how they learn. This develops over time by observing them carefully and by selecting planned strategies that will stimulate the children's participation by encouraging them in what they prefer to do.

And so the study is based on having the children learn primarily through play. In a play based curriculum, the staff support the children by understanding, then extending what they wish to do. They then resource the activities and develop strategies that will enhance their ability to play and learn. In this study play is the chosen way. Susan Isaacs explains that:

> Play is a child's life and, through play, children come to understand the world around them. (Isaacs 1937)

Surely this is the key aim for children who have yet to develop communication, empathy and altruism and as a result find the ways other children and adults behave confusing and unpredictable? And as they play, as they practise or initiate different play scenarios in a stress-free environment, the children learn to pretend and so begin to imagine events beyond the here and now. This leads to the children recognising that others have different feelings and emotions from them and so they begin to develop a theory of mind (ToM), a key competence in taking part in everyday social interactions. Play has also been shown to stimulate speech development in young children (Toth et al. 2006), so despite the intrinsic difficulties within autism and other conditions that house developmental delay in some or all aspects of development, there are increasingly recognised benefits of encouraging the children to learn through play.

During time at play, the staff observe to see if and how the children build social relationships with their peers and teachers and develop the motor skills, intellectual,

Figure 0.1 Is Jordan pretending?

social and emotional competences, i.e. the skills of daily living that will foster their self-awareness and lead to independence. Recording information about each child's participation and progress allows staff to plan interventions or justify non-interventions so that they work together to ensure the most appropriate learning opportunities occur. Hence Mastrangelo's (2009a) claim that:

> Play is not only a tool that prises open all areas of development and attempts to expand them; it is also a bridge between teacher and student.

Hopefully these bridges will promote bonding and trust.

The play-based method is quite different from what is sometimes described as a conditioning or behavioural method. The latter is based on adults breaking down a coping skill into discrete parts and showing and telling the children what to do, i.e. involving them in social training (SLT). In this method, the staff reward correct responses and they intend that this will lead to the more acceptable behaviour or competent skill being repeated. The reward, that can be a smile, a clap or a toy the child wishes to have, is given when the member of staff's request has been understood and fulfilled. Some children respond to this method very well. It can mean that the most efficient way to carry out a task is learned in the quickest time. Certainly Barry *et al.* (2003) found that both play skills and greeting skills improved when they were specifically taught. But while many parents and staff are delighted by the progress their children show, others explain they are uneasy with this intensive approach that is based on learning and rewarding specific coping skills.

On first reading this sounds very positive; the child is now able to use cutlery or copes with getting dressed – whatever competence has been taught. But a challenge arises when the child is not able to rationalise where the learned skill is appropriate. This is why opportunities for transfer of learning have been stressed in this book. Elizabeth, a teenager quite severely affected by autism, had learned to clear tables in her school setting. This was her special job and she did it with speed and skill. An evening out as a birthday treat, however, proved disastrous as before her carers had realised what was happening she had cleared the tables in the restaurant and all the cutlery was safely back in the drawers. All the tables had to be reset. The atmosphere was torrid!

An older child with high functioning autism (previously called Asperger's syndrome), Emily, having learned to swim and later visiting another pool for practice, asked the same teacher, 'Now can you teach me to swim in this pool?' Despite being at the able end of the autistic spectrum, she genuinely did not recognise the transferability of her success and imagined she would have to go through all the preliminary floundering around stages once more!

So, contextualisation and understanding the transfer of learning from one context to another is a real issue! This lack of ability to transfer learning so that a skill learned in one venue is used in another is hugely revealing. Parents in the study were sure that this was a critical impediment to learning for their child. They explained:

> Things the children learn stay in their own compartments. Things learned in school stay there as do things learned at home. When we say to the children, 'But you know how to do this', they look blank or upset and they have to be taught the skill again in the different place. Being able to get dressed in the morning at home does not seem to help getting dressed after gym, even when the same chart is available. Why should this be?

Because of this, parents and professionals in school can have a skewed picture of a child's progress that can lead to confusion. This shows the critical importance of detailed home/school communication and finding a way to break down any barriers that lack of transfer causes.

So, explanations and demonstrations about transferring learned skills will be required if the children's ability to use coping skills in each context is to be developed. Such progress must be monitored carefully because knowing how each child is progressing is critically important for enhancing the children's self-esteem and for developing the intrinsic motivation that leads to success in coping with the activities of daily living.

The different methods emphasise the importance of choosing what is appropriate for each child. Observing children at play can highlight a focus for a more specifically taught event and the acquisition of a new skill through more formal teaching can make more play scenarios possible. So the two strategies can complement each other, each playing a major or minor role so that the best educational outcome is achieved. The key aim is that the children will be more confident and competent and therefore happier, living in a busy, constantly changing world.

Developing verbal and non-verbal communication

One implicit difficulty within autism is that affected children may be slow to speak. Some children may have had early speech sounds but heartbreakingly this has disappeared and they must learn to communicate with other children and adults non-verbally i.e. using gestures or symbols, so that they can have a social life where they can express their needs and recognise that others need support too. How is this to be achieved? Here too there are different approaches that have to be matched to the children's different ways of learning.

Picture exchange system (PECS)

The successful PECS is a gentle method that leaves the children in control of selecting images/symbols to express their needs. The children begin by selecting just one symbol, e.g. a picture of a banana or an iPad. They pass this to an adult to show what they wish to have. Gradually, simple sentences are built as the children recognise text that says 'I want' and place this alongside a picture of what it is they need.

Especially with very young children, giving them a measure of communication and independence is very empowering. (When Jordan found he could use his PECS symbols to get what he wanted, he was enchanted, wanting something different all day long! He then had to learn to wait!) He soon calmed his requests, however, and began to be more selective. Was he considering the implications of asking for too much and learning to make choices? If so this was a significant gain.

Bondy (2012) has a few reservations. He explains that 'learning about the relationship between a picture and an object does necessarily teach the learner to direct a communicative act towards the listener'. To overcome this, staff have to be ready to follow, perhaps echo and thereafter elaborate the child's requests so as to establish the duo effect. He is also concerned if the system is used only with an 'I want' starter because in neurotypical children, not only do they have a rapid increase in vocabulary, they develop a more complex sentence structure. Staff using PECS, then, have not only to increase the number of pictures as the children develop recognition but consider the length and complexity of the sentence structure that could support them. The 'I can' phrase is a useful one for keeping track of achievements.

This can lead to a 'wall of achievement' (see Chapter 6) that is a colourful, ongoing, public and very impressive way of recognising progress.

Later, when the children are a little more independent and when difficulties arise they can use the symbol 'Help' as a means of communication. And because the children stay in control of what they want help for, this can complement the approach that favours children learning through play.

This done, Bondy (2012) found that in a controlled study, the PECS group made significant gains in communication and social domains that were stable after a year. And so his conclusion was that 'these findings demonstrated that PECS training can promote long-term enhancement of specific socio-communicative skills in children with autism'.

This system has its critics too, i.e. those who believe that reliance on symbols or signing, i.e. non-verbal means of communication will delay the acquisition of speech.

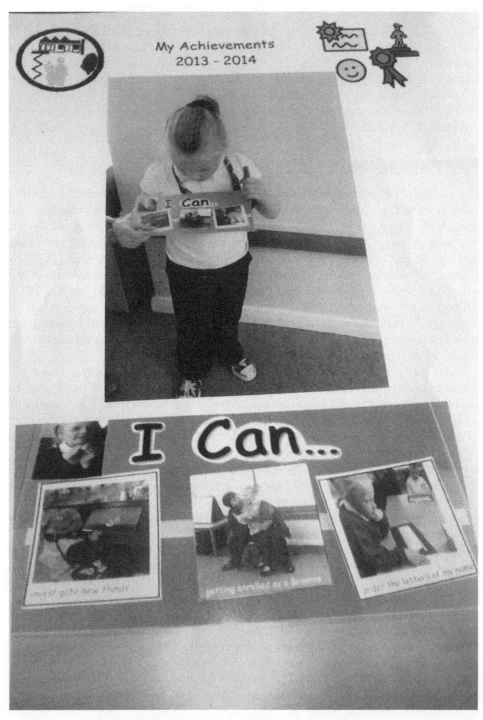

Figure 0.2 Susie shows her 'I can' board. Every child in the school has one and the symbols are changed regularly as new competences are achieved.

To counteract this, staff are careful to speak the words that the symbols represent as they are used. They do this so that the children will internalise the words that accompany the symbols and so begin the word recognition process that aids reading. This is similar to the 'look and say' method that has been found to be very successful with children with Down's syndrome. Some children, however, prefer signing.

Signing

Signing is a different method favoured by other professionals and parents. The signs are visually associated to the object to which they refer and so allow children to express themselves. Those who favour this method see this expression as *the* basis of promoting social interactions. Ricamato (2008) is one practitioner who claims gestures and signs stimulate communications that express meanings. He writes:

> It is always miraculous to see a child share experience and meaning with their caregiver through signs and more conventional gestures, demonstrating sheer joy at the power of communicating. It is even more miraculous to see many children who, when well supported in this manner, begin to verbally communicate in combination with gestures and signs.

So different methods have their followers and their critics. All of them, however, can have successful outcomes when the best method for the competence and preference of individual children is chosen. And of course the methods can be used together so that clarity is enhanced.

Building strategies to support the children

To ensure that each child makes progress, the staff must develop ways to observe, analyse and record what they see, then teach and interact in ways that match the learning status of each child in their care. Then, over time and with experience, they can build a bank of strategies to engage the children and stimulate their learning and their play. The concerns outlined above hint at the difficulties in 'getting it right' and explain why 'sharing strategies' is at the heart of this book. They provide ideas and 'starts' but professionals still need to amend them to fit their own situation and to match the abilities of their own children.

A further challenge to compiling a bank of strategies arises because there is not one 'typical' child who fits all the descriptors listed in the literature that describes different complex needs conditions. Although these provide general key issues and therefore give valuable starting points for observation, each observed child will be at a different place on the spectrum. Each will have subtle differences and preferences and these will affect what can be achieved. In addition, specific indicators can cross barriers and be part of several conditions. This is called co-occurrence. While this can blur the boundaries between different conditions causing diagnostic difficulties, it also means that the strategies designed to help children with one clutch of difficulties can support many more. It is also important to emphasise that no strategy will harm any child. And when a breakthrough occurs – and it will – the sense of achievement is wonderful. Parents, staff and the children themselves rejoice!

The study's next aim is to share positive, tried and tested strategies with more professionals so that they have a bank of ideas to support their children's learning. This will be done by sharing detailed case studies of a group of children of different ages and with different levels of needs so that readers can picture them, visualise their learning context and more fully appreciate the highs and lows, i.e. the reality of what went on.

Alongside these two key aims, the process of the investigation is explained. The question, 'In what ways can children's play provide useful observations so that with staff support they can develop competence in coping skills/activities of daily living?' suggests the cyclical and continuous action plan of observe, plan and evaluate the plan as it unfolds.

And so, through providing case studies, the text shares the ways in which the children were observed, explains how their progress was monitored and shows how strategies were compiled and evaluated. This is a book of practical ideas so that when professionals wonder, 'What can I do?', a bank of possibilities is at hand.

Why is this useful?

It is useful because a bank of strategies can be quickly retrieved and used as they stand or the ideas can be amended to suit different situations. The strategies have been sourced and trialled by a number of very experienced practitioners who have explained that 'just knowing you have something to try, something that has really helped the children' is an invaluable resource because you are never left floundering, thinking – sometimes very anxiously – 'What can I do now?'. Another group who collated, evaluated and shared the strategies claimed that 'even to know things were tried and didn't always work out stopped us feeling we had failed, and even when strategies sounded quite simple or when we had already tried similar things ourselves, reading

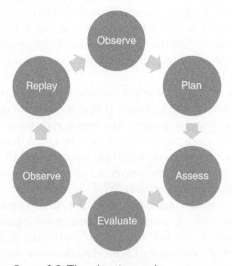

Figure 0.3 The planning cycle.

about them helped us realise we were on the right track and that gave us enough confidence to persevere and develop our ideas further'.

An extensive theoretical background (the theory chapters have strategies too) is given to show that the selection of strategies that were developed have a well-researched base. These strategies are not 'plucked from the sky'; they have been carefully chosen and justified so that the children have more chance of success. So explanations about critically important attributes (e.g. learning to crawl using the cross-lateral pattern; developing pointing to stimulate a 'joint initiative' or shared enterprise and so promoting communication; following rhythmical patterns in music; washing away retained primitive reflexes to allow postural reflexes to take their place; understanding sensory input and appreciating how some children are defeated by sensory overload and poor memorising skills; and very importantly learning to pretend) form a substantial part of the text. For if these competences fail to develop, then playing and learning and developing a theory of mind are all compromised. Strategies that can offer support and progress must surely be welcomed?

Teaching children with complex needs requires time to observe, to understand and to get into the minds of the children and follow their lead. Staff can feel frustrated when the children are slow to respond to carefully considered plans and it can be devastating if the children appear for a time to ignore people and plans and seem to regress to an earlier stage in their learning. But perhaps the children just need more time or perhaps something, even something outside school has happened to distress them? Or perhaps the teaching/playing plan doesn't match what the children prefer to do? Or it might just be that the children have an – often undisclosed and sometimes conflicting – plan all of their own? And often 'lost learning' can reappear later as if it had been waiting for the right time to emerge! Staff talk about 'a light suddenly getting switched on'. So learning is never wasted, it may be dormant for a while and then emerge!

When new strategies are gradually introduced, children with complex needs may not be able to communicate their pleasure or their distress by explaining what, in their view is right or wrong. They may not even understand it themselves. But the ideas may provide stimulation and alternative ways of playing and learning that intrigue the children and give a new focus to their day.

What sorts of breakthroughs are the team aiming to achieve?

They hope that the children will develop self-confidence by experiencing play activities where the team follow their lead and value their participation. As a result they may manage to do something they could not do before, e.g. they might learn to crawl, then to run and jump and kick a ball into a goal; they might be more accepting of small changes in their routine; they might gain confidence through achievement and praise: they might become more confident in playing in the outdoor classroom so developing their imaginations and their living skills.

N.B. The outdoor classroom needs as many resources as the indoor one!

And as they add to their repertoire of skills and understandings, hopefully they will find that this helps them appreciate what other children are doing and thinking. And so they begin to develop a theory of mind, i.e. understanding that others have different thoughts, preferences and needs to their own. Gradually they begin to develop altruism, perhaps through understanding the implications of what they do, e.g. they come to realise that if they push another child over, then that child can be hurt, or even retaliate! And so they might progress in each domain of learning, i.e. nurturing their motor/movement, intellectual, social and emotional skills. And this success might enable them to bond with their parents and their peers, be more confident with more people and be more willing to try new skills in different environments. Surely this is what teaching children with complex needs is all about?

A very special benefit for professionals, parents and other readers/observers is that they come to more fully understand the way children with ASC experience their world. Seeing the children as prime movers also means that the relationship changes. The children are the leaders while the professionals follow and guide. This way of teaching aims to convey to the children that their ideas and ploys are valued and worthy of respect. Hopefully this approach will nurture their self-esteem.

To teachers not experienced in working with children with very special needs, the aims and achievements outlined in this book might seem small, but consistently achieving small steps can make a big difference to a final outcome.

Boutot *et al.*'s (2005) plea was also a stimulus for this investigation. He wrote:

> More research is needed to determine which of several instructional approaches leads to the greatest gains in play skills as well as whether improvements in play skills has similar peripheral effects on language, motor and cognitive skills for children with autism as they do for typically developing children.

So let's begin!

Chapter 1

Come and meet our youngest children at play

First case studies with strategies to foster development

Come and meet some of our youngest children in their first year at school and find how the teaching strategies emerged from observing them closely to compile individual case studies as a basis for planning colourful play and more directed learning activities. The group of professionals who compiled the case studies is called 'the team'. Some members of the team have different specialisms/responsibilities, e.g. speech and language, physiotherapists and occupational therapists and they work with children throughout the school who need their particular expertise; art and physical education specialists teach all the children each week and smaller groups of classroom specialists, e.g. teachers and nursery nurses work with their own class of children every day. Together they monitor the children's progress and consider ideas for future development. They plan where play activities and more directed teaching would be appropriate and they provide a whole range of learning experiences, e.g. visiting a local canal and having snack on a barge, or going horse riding so that the children have a rich, varied education. Case studies of the children are shared so that the selection and implementation of strategies can be understood in the context where they took place.

In this opening chapter, you will meet Callum, Jacob, Kieran and Mia. These are four of the five-year-olds in the first class. Each case study gives an early description and a later one so that the children's reactions to the strategies are explained.

Case study for Callum who appears on the cover of the book

Callum is a gentle five-year-old who is severely affected by autism. This means that, at this time he has very poor communication skills and apart from one or two words, e.g. 'bubbles on', quietly but clearly offered in the sensory room, he doesn't choose to speak to make his needs known. Given this start, however, the team hope he is on the verge of saying more and will encourage this by finding what motivates him and quietly saying key words to accompany his play.

In class and generally around the school, Callum doesn't appear distressed; he rarely displays emotion. He just prefers wandering around or jumping up and down, two feet together with a bouncing action with (to the team) no apparent purpose. He often lies curled up face down on the floor, hiding his eyes and at times shielding his ears. This can indicate sensory hypersensitivity to both lights and sounds although auditory tests have found his level of hearing normal. He does move closely to the tubes of coloured bubbles in the sensory room and while this might suggest poor vision (which is tested) it could be that the sensations help fulfil his sensory needs. Watching the bubbles gives him a huge amount of pleasure – he is totally engrossed and still – yet he doesn't make a fuss when it is time to leave. He doesn't resist taking hands with members of the team, but he doesn't offer any eye contact either – he looks straight ahead.

In the classroom he seems intrigued by the ceiling. The team wonder whether it is the pattern made by incoming light and why this area should hold his interest. Perhaps he wants to avoid the colourful visual displays that adorn the walls? Or perhaps, as his very experienced nursery nurse, Gemma, described him, 'he is a child of squares and shadows'. She had observed Callum running his fingers along the edges of the door and choosing hard plastic bricks, not to build but just to feel the hard edges. He also appears entranced by the shadows made by the branches of the tree in the playground and will sway mirroring their action. Is he a visual thinker? Does his learning rely on visual images? It will be intriguing to find if Callum registers whole pictures or begins by absorbing details and builds them into pictures. Grandin (2014) in *The Autistic Brain* has one chapter called 'Rethinking in pictures' where she differentiates between the visual images children see and the perceptions others have. When Callum learns to speak he will be able to explain if he is asked the right questions. Meanwhile the team observe him carefully and gather data to try to explain the way Callum's thinking is expressed in his actions.

In the soft play room, he appears interested in pictures on the wall and will stand facing them, jumping up and down rather than being involved in free play on the soft apparatus. In class, he has a favourite plastic toy, a torch, and he walks around with this held closely to his ear. It emits a quiet sound interspersed with a soft count of 1, 2, 3, 4, 5. Carol, the occupational therapist, suggests that Callum listening to the soft sound may help him cut out the other noises in the room. If this is so, he has found a useful way to reduce any sensory overload. He *will* put the toy down though, so although it seems to comfort him, it is not an obsession – he is not fixated on having it, nor does he appear upset if another child has a turn.

At 'circle time', a time for joining together to sing the 'hello' song, listen to a story or to follow the visual timetable that indicates what activity comes next, he will sit down for brief spells but shows no animation towards any song or story. He follows the classroom routine; he copes with hand washing, teeth cleaning and visiting the toilet; he makes no fuss at all. Although he makes very little eye contact with the staff, he can fix his eyes on items he wants to have. Even then his facial expression doesn't change.

Fortunately he enjoys his food (many children with autism are very picky eaters) and he will point to his favourite item on the snack table – a banana. He clutches this and moves away. As yet, he is using an adult as a tool rather than someone to share experiences but the fact that he points is encouraging for this can herald communication that in time can stimulate speech. Callum is newly able to find the picture of a banana in his PECS book that contains a number of velcro fastened symbols and the team is working to have him recognise and use the 'I want' symbol so that a short sentence can be made.

For a good part of the day he prefers to be isolated and silent. He is not aggressive to other children but on occasion can become so frustrated that he bangs his head on the floor or pulls his hair hard. Very occasionally he will nip a child who comes too close, but this is reducing as he gains confidence in his surroundings. The other children often smile at him and are happy to sit by him, but his lack of response means he is often alone.

Out of doors he fills in time but couldn't be said to be playing with any purpose or gaining much motor development in terms of strength or control. He avoids the cycles and floor trampoline and he stumbles quite often, suggesting that his sense of balance is underdeveloped. He has some hyper-flexibility in his hips and low muscle tone in his legs, perhaps due to his unwillingness to run around, so outdoor play is very important for him. His fine motor skills, e.g. using the pincer grip are, not yet fully developed either. He will pick up a crayon, clutching it rather than using the pincer grip, but he has no interest in mark making. His hand dominance is still to be established for although he usually carries his toy in his left hand, he uses his right one to feed himself at snack and lunch times. Banana is his favourite, with crackers and hummus second. He prefers savoury finger foods to yoghurt and jelly. It is quite difficult to encourage him to have milk or juice but he will have water.

When he does pick up a toy, he spins it round and round and if thwarted, e.g. by suggestions or demonstrations of other ways to use it, he ignores these and wanders away. He likes to line up the small toys but doesn't appear to differentiate between bricks and animals – he doesn't give them personalities.

He is not yet toilet trained. Callum's parents explain that he is a poor sleeper. This leaves the family exhausted.

What can we do? Two strategies to develop Callum's skills

Ellie, Callum's nursery nurse was instrumental in his development. She was anxious to build on Callum's existing actions so her written aims were just one step ahead of his present level of development. In this way they could be attainable and recorded as progress.

1) She wanted to extend his purposeful pointing skills so that he came to understand communication and realised that adults could help him have things he could not reach alone. She hoped that communication would stimulate bonding and also that Callum would come to appreciate when seeking help was appropriate.

2) She also wished to teach him to crawl using the cross lateral pattern. He already crouched on the floor so Ellie decided to use that as a starter and encourage him to stretch his limbs and balance on his hands and knees in the table position. This would help to strengthen his legs and his pelvic area so that crawling using the cross lateral pattern, with all its intrinsic gains, became possible.

Strategies

a) Ellie explained how she developed Callum's skills. She began by using his liking for banana! First of all, Ellie realised that Callum had to see the banana before he wanted it – he did not appear to think, 'I feel like having a piece of banana' and then search for it. The sight stimulated the desire. She explained her thinking behind her action plan,

I built on his liking for bananas by placing them where he could see them but just out of his reach. He had then to realise that I could help him so I showed him how this could happen. The next move was that I stayed back so that he had to come for me and point to the banana. I said the word 'banana' quietly as he looked for help. I also demonstrated that he could fetch the 'I want' picture from his PECS book and show that to anyone in the room. Having a piece of banana was his reward. Very quickly Callum came to realise that I was willing to help him and appeared pleased when he achieved his goal. I tried to hold eye contact but he was only focusing on the banana at this time.

Ellie hoped this 'shared enterprise' would build up trust and communication.

b)   As Callum did not look around for objects that were not immediately visible, Ellie placed the banana on a shelf but slightly to the side so that Callum would have to select a PECS symbol then begin to search. Gradually as Callum followed this new routine she increased the distance so that Callum would come to recognise that objects out of sight could still be there.

c)   Ellie then tried to interest Callum in peek-a-boo games to encourage communication through turn taking, but also to give him practice in realising that people or objects could still be present even if they were covered or out of sight. This was to develop object permanence, however Callum appeared baffled by this and lost interest quickly.

What did Callum learn?

Intellectual/social skills

Callum has quite quickly grasped the idea that Ellie will help him. After three weeks, he is more confident in using his PECS symbols to contact Ellie to get pieces of banana. He recognises that the two dimensional picture symbolises the actual fruit.

He is searching for and recognising words in his PECS book, e.g. crackers, toast. Ellie hopes that this is a sign that he will soon ask for other things.

He is willing to contact other adults for support.

Motor skills

He is using the pincer grip to detach and manipulate the PECS symbol. This should help inhibit his palmar reflex and so make his finger and hand movements more precise.

Forward plan

a)   Try to extend this shared initiative idea by having him point to a glass of water and then use two symbols, the first for 'I want,' the second for 'a drink'.

b)   Put his toy on the shelf just out of reach so that he has to search and come for help. This would show he was able to transfer his learning to encompass different items.

This plan followed the advice given by Barrett *et al.* (2004) who wrote, 'Look for opportunities to organise the environment so that a child can experience success in achieving a goal with help from an adult, i.e. try to develop "shared initiatives"'.

Social skills

Two weeks later, Callum used the 'I want' symbol to get support from two adults although they were not able to discover what it was he wanted. Perhaps he just wanted attention? The fact that he approached them showed he was recognising that he could cooperate with a chosen adult. He was initiating contact. This was a real step forward and another encouraging instance of *transfer* of learning for he had realised that 'help' did not always mean bananas!

Emotional skills

The team hoped that he had gained confidence, as he was more willing to approach adults to make his wishes known. His overtures also resulted in successes e.g. knowing he could request what he wanted. The team hoped that 'being in charge' through making choices would boost his self-esteem and give him a measure of independence.

Theoretical link: 'Milieu teaching'

Garfinkle and Schwartz (2002) call this kind of interaction, 'Milieu teaching', i.e. taking advantage of teachable moments by setting up the environment so that these moments were likely to re-occur. They explain that this approach has been used successfully even with preschool children with autism. In addition, 'verbal modelling', i.e. 'the teacher making comments or asking questions that have come from observing the child's play and teaching specific skills can be embraced within this strategy' (Boutot *et al.* 2005). This was important as the team aimed to stimulate Callum's play skills.

Strategy 2: Developing crawling using the cross lateral pattern

This was a different kind of intervention because although Callum curled up tightly, face down on the floor, he had shown no interest in crawling or moving in any direction. Perhaps he was hiding or cutting out noise? Whatever the reason, he resisted any encouragement from his teacher, Laura, to move. So this action plan involved more directed teaching. This was because Laura was anxious that he learned to crawl using the cross lateral pattern. She knew that homolateral crawling or bum shuffling would not have the same beneficial effects and that if this pattern became established it would be difficult to change.

What were these benefits?

Laura was following Goddard's (2002) advice that using the cross lateral pattern (one hand then the opposite knee going forward) is very important for developing not only coordination and the ability to cross the midline of the body but also visual acuity.

This is because during the crawling movement, the eyes follow the hands as they move forward, going from side to side. Any visual gain was particularly appropriate for Callum. The team also knew that the homo lateral pattern adopted by many children (i.e. hands and knees on the same side going forward together) possibly showed a retained reflex that prevented the more sophisticated cross lateral pattern being adopted. If this happened, it meant that there could be difficulties in many everyday activities that involved crossing the midline of the body, e.g. in getting dressed, turning pages in a book, even using a knife and fork at table. Very importantly Goddard (2002) also claimed that, 'taking the children back through basic activities such as crawling would cause new neural pathways in the brain to be formed and so give the brain a second chance'.

Strategy

a) Following this recommendation, the headteacher immediately brought clear plastic tunnels to crawl through into the playground hoping they would motivate the children's curiosity, set up a new challenge and give them all the opportunity to relearn basic skills. The team crawled through the tunnel to reassure the children that it was fun. Children who didn't want to do this could have fun rolling balls through. The team watched this and helped the children develop it into a game, one child rolling the ball, the other collecting it and rolling it back. In this way cooperation was encouraged and the team hoped that when the children saw the balls come safely through, this would give them the confidence to try crawling through themselves.

b) Laura tried to encourage Callum to lift his body from the curled position, i.e. to extend his arms and legs into the table position (i.e. with a flat back well supported on four limbs) as a preparation for crawling. The other children were either learning to crawl or developing their skill by crawling over or through different 'obstacles' such as piles of cushions and the tunnel brought indoors. He had a visual demonstration but didn't seem impressed. The teacher was also crawling alongside him on the floor to encourage him to move from the spot. At first, this didn't work – Callum showed no interest in the crawling activity and so the team decided to try another day rather than try to force the issue. Callum watched the others with half an eye and the team hoped that he would internalise something of the action.

What skills were developed?

Motor skills

Crawling: at first, this was not successful and the action plan had to be amended. Laura and nursery nurse Natalie then took Callum back through the preliminary stages of learning to crawl, e.g. pulling along the floor to reach his favourite toy then pushing arms straight to look up. This was to strengthen his arms, neck and shoulders. Callum was able to do this. Then he pulled both legs up and stretched both hands forward. Some time later he coped with a rocking action moving his weight from feet to hands and back again, then he curled up again. This did not involve the rhythm or the cross lateral pattern but it was a start. This was also a balance practice in the secure table position.

Further information on sensory integration, pointing as communication, the importance of crawling using the cross lateral pattern, reflexes and their influence on learning, is given in Chapter 3.

Callum, nine months later – an account written by Ellie, Callum's nursery nurse, Gemma, Natalie and Laura

> Callum can now request various items using his PECS symbols. He has moved beyond the initial exchange (handing over the symbol for a particular object) and uses a sentence strip, e.g. I want . . . banana, biscuit, torch etc. He will now come and find members of staff, show his sentence strip and persist till his needs are met. The object he wishes to have no longer needs to be within his sight for him to request it; he now initiates communication spontaneously. Callum now appears more comfortable with the class routine and is able to follow simple instructions and gestures e.g. Come to the snack table please.

Recently, Callum has shown interest in the visual timetable when it is explained at morning circle. He points to symbols such as soft play and snack. He is beginning to give more eye contact to staff (albeit for brief periods) and very occasionally initiates some interaction with peers when in areas he now enjoys (soft play and more recently the gym hall). In the gym he is happiest running around in the big space. As yet he doesn't really take part in the lesson but he is now willing to sit on the bench to listen to instructions. He runs and jumps, still on his own but at least he has some beneficial activity. He is just beginning to be interested in what the other children are doing, e.g. he watched them throwing beanbags over a bench to land on the floor on the other side whereupon another child had to throw them back, the aim of the game being to keep the floor on their own side clear. Was Callum becoming interested in the coloured beanbags or the throwing action? Was the scuffle of children collecting the beanbags putting him off joining in? It was hard to know!

When Callum gets really anxious, e.g. at morning assembly, he will request time in the sensory room to watch the rising bubbles and be calmed. 'Bubbles on' is still his favourite instruction. Outdoors he stands by the tunnels and he is just beginning to venture inside. He carries his yellow bricks wherever he goes now, stroking the edges and feeling the corners. The team feel his confidence is growing as he walks without so much stumbling and overbalancing and in 1:1 teaching sessions he is beginning to be able to use the pincer grip to complete his wooden jigsaw. The team is delighted by his progress.

N.B. When Mrs Rosie, the headteacher, saw how many children were enjoying crawling through the tunnels and appreciating the many benefits of crawling, she purchased the caterpillar which provided balancing opportunities as well as lengthy crawling ones! Look at Callum on the cover of the book. Interestingly, he has taken his precious bricks inside. Crawling so far using the cross lateral pattern is a big achievement! He does not appear fazed by the length of the tunnel or the dim inside. Laura's earlier teaching that didn't seem to work at the time has surfaced some time later and delighted us all!

But could he be said to be playing? His activities, to our eyes still seem to lack focus but then play needn't be purposeful. He is engrossed, so we hope he enjoys what he is doing. When clapping followed his emergence from the tunnel there was a moment of animation. He has developed communication skills through using PECS and the team hope that moments of stillness and focus are signs that speech will follow. Is he pretending? We don't know.

Case study for Jacob

Jacob is newly five. He is bright-eyed and lively and anxious to be involved in anything that is going on. At this moment in time he has very little speech although he understands everything that is said. He listens to stories and is able to match pictures of the characters in a recap book some time afterwards, showing that he remembers from one day to the next. Generally he understands and is willing to follow instructions in class and in the playground. However, he can become over-boisterous, especially in the soft play area. If there is a slight bump or if another child is on 'his' equipment, he can retaliate using too much strength and the staff divert the others till he has regained composure. He doesn't seem to realise that they might be hurt. He also likes to be 'in charge' and it can be hard for him to give another child a turn. In class, at choosing time he commandeers the laptop, shrugs off any offers of help and gets frustrated and angry when his idea of the password doesn't work. He is motivated and purposeful!

His use of language and PECS are developing slowly but surely. His body language signals that he is happy and he is always busy. As yet, he stays with functional play, throwing balls into hoops and doesn't show any sign of pretending. The team showed a video of a basketball game because of the similar skills being used in a major game but this didn't hold his attention.

Strategy: the team will set up opportunities for pretending, e.g. instead of matching characters from a story they will involve Jacob in action ploys, e.g. in Jack and the Beanstalk, he will gather up beans and carry them home; he will cut down the beanstalk and take giant steps (see *Jingle Time* (Macintyre 2003) for a 'Giant' poem). They will contrast this with little children scampering to hide. This introduces expressive vocabulary in a play setting.

The feelings of the characters will be highlighted in simple ways, e.g. the giant was grumpy because the children woke him up. Let's all look grumpy . . . and so on.

Jacob's favourite ploy is tidying the classroom, wiping tables and lining up chairs. He recognises that in class, the 'tidy-up song' signals that it is time to begin putting things in order and he is always anxious to begin. This is a purposeful activity that gives Jacob satisfaction and the team decided to follow him and try to expand his interest, where possible explaining how his actions can transfer to home events and thus develop useful activities of daily living.

Strategy for taking the idea forward: take the P.E. lesson outdoors and provide resources to develop play. Emphasise transfer of learning

a) The idea of how to develop this idea came from a colour recognition lesson in the gym. The specialist P.E. teacher Sam explained to the children that she was being

Figure 1.1 Jacob and Mia are engrossed in tidying the playground. They are working together to achieve this. They have a real job!

'untidy' throwing small rubber hoops and beanbags all over the floor. Some were red and others were green. All the children had to run to gather them up and place them in the large hoop of the same colour. After the teacher giving a demonstration showing what was to happen, Jacob understood the instructions. Although he made no contact with the other children he smiled and seemed to enjoy scuttling around and gathering and placing the hoops and beanbags 'tidily' in the large hoops. He identified the colours correctly.

b)   The game was transferred to the outside area, the playground, and as it was September, Jacob was able to sweep leaves and shovel them into a large bin. The similarity to the gym lesson was explained. 'Look we are tidying up the yard just like we tidied up the hoops and beanbags in the gym'. This was to help him to understand the transfer of learning.

Resources

A number of sweeping brushes and some shovels were laid out in the playground and a large waste paper bin was placed centrally.

Reaction

When he heard about keeping the playground tidy, Jacob was first to run outside. He grabbed the largest hard brush to sweep up the leaves. This was a strengthening activity that would develop the muscles in his arms and shoulders. The team scattered some extra cardboard litter to make the job 'heavier' and to give an alternative to leaves that are light and floaty. They used some new language, e.g. sweeping up, shovelling, and emphasised the similarities to the indoor lesson.

After some time sweeping energetically and becoming frustrated with leaf gathering on a windy day, Jacob abandoned his brush and gathered the leaves and litter in his arms and placed it in the bin. He had understood the concept and demonstrated his understanding of the task. He was given a round of applause! This was real problem-solving.

The team were able to claim that play and work had blended together into a useful activity of daily living. In Ingersoll *et al.*'s (2010) terms, this was functional play. Jacob was carrying out a task; he was pleased by the praise, but as far as the team knew he was not pretending.

Strategy 2

The team placed an assortment of brushes and some shovels out of sight in a hut in the playground. Would Jacob remember and repeat his task? Jacob could choose a hard brush for sweeping up stones or a smaller softer one for small cartons and other junk. After some experimentation he recognised which brush was best for each job. He also had to gauge the amount of strength needed for the task. The teacher repeated the word 'sweep' as he worked and although he did not manage to repeat it, he was listening and mouthing the sound, hopefully in preparation for speaking the word later.

What was Jacob gaining/learning?

Motor skills

1) General strengthening through controlling a heavy brush. This particularly strengthened his shoulders. His *spatial awareness* was challenged through adjusting his stance to accommodate the sweeping action.
2) His coordination was developed through working out how to use two pieces of weighty equipment, i.e. the brush and shovel at the same time.
3) He was fulfilling a *balance challenge* in gathering the leaves and litter onto the shovel then into the bin. This was a difficult sequence of activity that required perseverance especially when the wind blew the leaves.
4) This was also a '*crossing the midline activity*' that would assist page turning indoors and getting dressed at home and after gym. Observations of Jacob sweeping and especially holding the shovel, showed that he had achieved *hand dominance*.

Intellectual skills

1) Making decisions about when to sweep (waiting for the wind to drop) and choosing the most appropriate brush for the task.

2) Completing a task that was a useful activity of daily living and one that earned him a sticker that said 'Well done.'
3) Learning how hard work affected his body and how a cold drink could refresh him.

Social skills

This was mainly a solitary activity focusing on the sweeping and gathering actions but other children watched and in the picture Mia shows she is anxious to help.

Action plan: develop this into a cooperative activity when other children have brushes and shovels too. Emphasise 'We are all working together to clear the playground'. The children were allowed into the 'big children's playground' to tidy up there, so they were helping others. The older children came to class to say 'Thank you'.

Emotional skills

Self-confidence gained in completing a hard job!

Discussion and debate: transferring learning: resourcing the learning environment.

Before the strategies were tried, the team was anxious to find if so many new resources might confuse Jacob, but he appeared to relish having the brushes and a real job! The lesson in the gym had provided a base and the opportunity for explaining and experiencing transfer of learning, i.e. using similar skills in different environments.

The question of having a very calm ordered environment with no distractions has been recommended for children with autism for some time. The American Son Rise programme that makes very significant claims about clearing the barriers of autism, is adamant that 'a distraction free space' and intensive practice in that space is essential for the children's concentration and learning to be nurtured. Yet this seems to be changing, perhaps because although the children do learn skills and words to describe them, they do not appreciate transfer so do not see the relevance of using the skill elsewhere (this was raised by the parents as a key limitation). In contrast, authors such as Lynn Young from the University of California make a very significant point. She claims that:

> An enriched sensory – motor environment ameliorates genetically based neurological disorders.

This is important in justifying providing a range of resources that provide more opportunities to practise playing and especially if transfer is explained, becoming more competent in the activities of daily living.

This strategy had transferred essentially the same activity from indoors in the gym to the outdoor setting. Jacob appeared to grasp the transfer as he immediately began tidying. But did he appreciate this or was it just another activity? As transfer of learning is now a key point for observing learning, the team considered that opportunities like this should be planned and the transfer, or similarities in tasks should be explained to the children, not once but every time the opportunity arose.

N.B. Discussions with parents endorsed the claim that transfer of learning was a key factor in assessing children's progress. They explained that their children seemed to think that a skill learned in one environment belonged only there. One parent, caring for four children, all on the spectrum, was sure that 'transfer' was critically important:

> If the children could only appreciate transferring learning from one place to another, think how much repetition that would save. That's important for the children but it would ease so much frustration for us parents too. No matter how much we care, we get so tired saying the same things over and over again. Understanding transfer is the key. I do believe that.

Reflection

The team decided to make this a priority and revisited curriculum plans to understand how separate ideas could be linked, e.g. the team had envisaged that the children would recognise the relationship between buying items in the classroom shop and going to the local store but now they questioned that and made transfer a concrete aim, e.g. if the children put six china eggs in a box in class, the team ensured they purchased six real eggs in the shop, took them back to the class and compared these to the china ones before taking them to the kitchen.

Speaking

Suddenly and to everyone's delight Jacob volunteered, 'Mia is not here today'. Quiet words had been heard before but this sentence dumbfounded everyone!

Case study for Kieran

In class, Kieran settles in the learning circle readily. He is usually quiet but he has some language and, when asked directly, he will quietly respond with a few words. He rarely initiates communication but seems to be absorbing stories and he can whisper-count up to ten. He enjoys 'phonics games' and will often offer a correct sound without being asked, e.g. he would volunteer 'sssss' as he played with a rubber snake. He listens to a short story intently and patiently and can identify characters on a matching chart some time later. He will answer a question about the story next day, showing he can remember. He is a very obedient, pleasant child, never aggressive or sulky. He goes to the gym and other out of classroom activities willingly. He under-stands the routine of the day through using the visual timetable and he is beginning to appreciate 'now' and 'next'. He is not yet toilet trained. The team feel 'there is a lot going on' in Kieran's mind and try to find ways to give him the confidence to show it.

He tolerates the other children but doesn't yet offer any verbal or even non-verbal communication – perhaps because their responses are not always forthcoming. He appears content, in many ways a perfect pupil.

Surprisingly perhaps, he is always ready to rush outdoors where he 'drives' the large tricycle that has been adapted to have two back seats for passengers and is generally known as 'the bus'. Despite non-verbal gestures by the team suggesting they join him, some of the other children are not interested in being driven around the playground. One or two make tentative overtures suggesting they would like to sit in the back seats but they shy away from any offer of help to get in. They don't have the confidence or the motor skills to move into place. Perhaps they are afraid that Kieran will drive off before they have time to sit, perhaps they are unsure of the speed or Kieran's ability to turn corners safely. Perhaps the close proximity to another child is too confining? However, other children do enjoy being passengers especially if an adult is there to control the speed.

Extending Kieran's play

As he has room for two passengers on the 'bus' the team decided to try to extend his play in line with experiences he would encounter when he travelled on the bus to town with his parents. This would support his transfer of learning skills.

Strategy 1

a) On day one, Gemma provided a driver's hat for Kieran. He really enjoyed this. On day two some laminated 'bus tickets' were made and Kieran was to give them to his passengers. This took some persuasion! The other children who wished to

Figure 1.2 Kieran, pretending to be the bus driver, enjoys being in charge.

Figure 1.3 The children develop social communication through exchanging tickets. They are enjoying and understanding their game.

be passengers had some plastic coins to pay their fare. (This was over-ambitious – the children would not wait). The team hoped that the 'exchange' would stimulate a means of communication and for Kieran this was a chance to establish one-to-one correspondence. By this time there were children anxious to become passengers. (Leon watched from the sideline, crouching low then gently took his seat as a passenger. He didn't make any overtures to the other passengers or the driver but took his ticket and sat down without any change of expression. This was a huge step forward for Leon to get involved in what was essentially parallel rather than isolate play. The next development was to have a bell fixed on the handlebars to tell other children to stand clear.)

b)   Next, a bus stop was set up, but sometimes the bus didn't stop when requested and as class teacher Laura explained, 'poor Rob was left waiting with his arm stretched out while the bus sailed past'. Then a parking place was drawn on the tarmac. After the journey or when a child wished to leave the bus, then the tickets were to be placed in the waste bin. Then the driver had to park the bus in the correct place (marked lines on the ground) rather than abandoning it to run indoors.

This was a complicated activity challenging Kieran's understanding of sequences; it was based on developing his choice of play activity and the team hoped to extend his communication skills through becoming aware of the part the other children were playing in the game. Kieran had to recognise when they wanted to leave the bus. Ringing the bell helped his fine motor skills, looking out for waiting passengers was to help develop communication and empathy and having to park the bus carefully established the end of the game.

There was a balance of functional play in this activity with many opportunities to develop imaginative play or pretence.

What was Kieran learning?

Intellectual skills

1) Distributing tickets to each passenger so developing the mathematical skill of one-to-one correspondence.
2) Recognising the word 'STOP' and slowing the bus in time. Developing anticipation of what comes next.
3) Developing planning and sequencing skills – remembering what comes first and next.
4) Taking the role of the driver, he was learning to pretend (simple pretence) but anticipating the wishes of the other children needed advanced pretend.

Motor skills

1) Cycling (strengthening legs and arms).
2) Coordination: ringing the bell while the bus was moving. Controlling the direction of the bus.
3) Slowing the bus and turning corners safely with passengers aboard.
4) For passengers there was 'motor decision-making' in deciding how, when and where to move while getting on and off the bus. This developed their spatial awareness and timing skills.

Social skills

1) Increased communication between driver and passengers.
2) Skill in waiting at the bus stop with other passengers; turn taking; waiting patiently for a ticket.

Emotional skills

1) Kieran was 'in charge' and relishing this opportunity. The team hoped he would become more confident and prompted his pretending by asking, e.g. 'Is this bus going to the shops? What will we buy there? Have we enough petrol?'
2) They also looked to develop empathy by suggesting, 'Poor Tom (a sailor doll) has a sore head. Let's drive him to hospital. We'll have to go slowly and carefully'.

DISCUSSION

There was some consternation within the team that Kieran had taken over the bus and was becoming rumbustious! He was reluctant to be a passenger and tried to pull another child out of the driver's seat. Both children were upset and so the bus disappeared into the shed till things calmed down!

The transfer of learning was explained by the team reminding Kieran of his experience on the school bus, coming to school and going home.

The team had decided views on removing the bus. While some explained that it created turmoil, others considered that removing it was wasting an opportunity to learn about sharing and turn taking. The compromise, i.e. to have the bus out on alternate days meant that understanding the sequence of learning new things, e.g. queuing, reading the notice 'Bus Stop,' having a turn, sometimes as driver but being gracious as a passenger, took a little longer.

Case study for Mia

Mia is a very lively five-year-old who beams a welcome when people she knows comes into class so she comes over as a very engaging child. However, although she has immediate eye contact, she is easily diverted and finds it difficult to sustain communication. She has ADHD (attention deficit hyperactivity disorder) so is on medication that has a calming effect. This makes her day more settled and she can learn more, although the team realise that when the medication wears off, or if she hasn't taken it at home (she can problem-solve ways to avoid taking it!), she is less able to be in control. As yet, she has just a few unclear spoken words but she is trying to say more. Interestingly, although she rarely speaks, she was determined that the team should know that 'Greg' had hurt her arm and her non-verbals, i.e. clutching her forearm and frowning left the adults in no doubt that she was angry. She repeated 'Greg' several times, a hard word for a child with little speech. This showed that she remembered and that she could display emotions – would that help her to recognise them in others, e.g. on live faces or in pictures?

Mia enjoys attention and can be very demanding. Physically she is very strong even although she has a slight build and it can be difficult to get back any items she has decided to 'lightning-grab.' She particularly enjoys purses with cards and phones, preferably purloined from someone's handbag! She appears to bear no malice after a tussle to retrieve these things; she just moves on to something else. Unfortunately although she can make her wants known, she very quickly loses interest in whatever she has yearned for. This makes it very difficult to engage her interest in stories or songs. She still walks on her toes for a part of each day. She can also build strategies to get her own way. Could this be called problem-solving?

For whatever reason she doesn't seem to enjoy the soft play area, so after telling everyone 'shoes off' at the door, she decides she needs the toilet. 'Wee Wee' is part of her limited vocabulary. That involves her in getting her coat and shoes on again and crossing the playground back into the main school so it takes some time. If Natalie, the nursery nurse who has just taken Mia to the toilet in school, suspects she is having them on and tries to divert her attention, she wets the floor! Then soft play has to stop! She has developed her own strategy for getting out of things she doesn't want to do, however it is important for the development of her vestibular system (balance) that she gets involved in what Orr (2003) calls 'rough and tumble play'. So somehow the staff must have her realise that her ploys don't always work. Her large, sparkling brown eyes and wide smiles make this very difficult.

She is aware of the other children and appears upset (she turns away clutching her arms around her middle and looks distressed) if one gets bumped. So she is empathising with other children. She remembers too! One boy pulled her hair and she mimed this, (pulling her own hair accompanied by growling whenever she saw him) for some considerable time!

At snack and lunch she eats quite well particularly enjoying baked potatoes with cheese and yoghurt. (As her medication can dull her appetite, a close watch has to be kept on her weight). However if she wants away from the table and others are not ready she will deliberately tip her milk over the table. The team's policy is to tidy the mess away without making a fuss so hopefully she will desist! Her ADHD causes her to be impetuous so she is never scolded for something she cannot help. What can the team do to help her become more patient?

Strategy 1

A first try was to give Mia a toy fluffy kitten that she hadn't seen before. The idea was that with her nursery nurse she would stroke it gently and rhythmically and so she would engage in a calming activity. The team hoped this would also develop the empathy she had shown towards others. The short ditty was to be intoned as she stroked.

> 'Softly, softly, stroke a little kitten,
> Gently, gently, gently stroke its fur,
> Quietly, quietly, you don't want to get bitten
> Listen to it purr.'

> (One of the rhymes in *Jingle Time*,
> Macintyre (2003))

Sadly, Mia was not interested in the kitten at all. She grabbed it and threw it across the room!! And when 'Oh, poor kitten' was exclaimed, she just stomped off. She did look back to gauge the team's reaction so they vowed to try this another time, perhaps when she was tired at the end of the day and more able to settle.

Strategy 2

Mia does love handbags, phones and purses that belong to the staff so the next strategy was to prepare a handbag full of articles for her to see if that made her feel special – there were no other girls in the class. In the handbag there was a small brush and comb, a mirror, a purse with plastic 'cards', a pen and some coins. Mia astounded the staff by delving into the bag and very clearly requesting, 'make-up!' Again motivation helped her to speak. Moreover, here was a child who could transfer ideas from home because there was no make-up at school and no-one realised she knew what it was. So what was she learning?

Intellectual skills

The next day she looked for and laid claim to the bag and purse and took out the cards before going to the classroom shop, so she was beginning to understand exchanging plastic for goods.

Fine motor skills

Mia was keen to pull the cards from the purse and replace them. This was fiddly and she persevered for a time before abandoning the task. This helped develop her pincer grip. She took the other articles from the bag but after a cursory glance appeared uninterested.

Strategy 3

Since Mia was able to recognise emotions in other children and could problem-solve, the next stage was to see if she could empathise with characters from a story. The team chose 'Goldilocks and the Three Bears' because of the linked activities, e.g. walking quietly through the forest, cooking porridge for the three bears and pretending to cry like baby bear when he discovered his porridge was all eaten up.

Strategy: developing the story of the three bears and moving from simple to advanced pretend.

The first idea was to have the children make and taste porridge. Did you know that Scotland has a porridge day in December? This was followed by the children feeding the three bears because they were hungry and the children did this enthusiastically with much enjoyment. This activity complemented a literacy activity where the children selected PECS cards to place under pictures of Goldilocks and the three differently sized and dressed bears.

SIMPLE PRETEND

This enjoyable activity involved the children in simple pretend. They pretended to feed the bear but this could be simply carrying out a task rather than appreciating how the bear was feeling or if he was happier after his meal.

DEVELOPING ADVANCED PRETEND (THEORY OF MIND)

This episode was followed up by suggesting that the greedy bear had eaten too much porridge and had a sore tummy. Everyone rubbed their tummies and groaned. One or two of the children stayed by the bear, rubbing its fur to comfort it. They appeared to empathise with its pain!

This story and play activity worked well together and the children returned to their collage of the house in the wood with Goldilocks and the three bears, hopefully remembering the sequence of activities that they had enjoyed.

Figure 1.4 Is Mia understanding that the bear will feel better after his meal?

Figure 1.5 Mia solves the problem of Bear being full up!

Strategy 4 Walking and running. Scouts pace.

Out of doors, Mia loves running and will happily take a member of staff for a run round the playground. The new activity was to alternate walking and running in a rhythmical pattern, like scouts pace, saying 'walking slowly' and 'running quickly' to emphasise the difference in speed. The hope was that understanding 'slowly' might help transfer the change of pace to her other work. She is almost cycling the trike but again her very short attention span prevents much progress.

Mia's 'best success' was sustaining involvement with the Goldilocks story. For this she was made 'star of the week'. She beamed with delight and tried to say 'Mummy', showing that she was anxious to share her success at home.

Each week one child in each class is made 'star of the week' and is presented with a trophy at Friday assembly.

ADHD

Mia shows all the characteristics of the condition ADHD, i.e. lack of concentration, short attention span and physical restlessness. Imaging studies show that affected children have an underlying neurological dysfunction. Carter (2000) explains that the children's control centres in their brains 'have yet to come fully on line'. While the limbic system is working strongly, the cortical areas which focus attention, control impulses and integrate stimuli are not fully active. So fixing attention, controlling impulses and planning actions are all affected. Medication stimulates the under active areas, helping concentration and allowing more focused behaviour. This condition should improve as the children mature, i.e. when the reward centres in the brain are more fully activated.

Before then, professionals are urged to redefine these children so that their difficulties are seen in a more positive light and they are not blamed for something they simply cannot help.

Table 1.1 Redefining children with ADHD

Negative thoughts	Positive alternatives
Being out of seat too much	Energetic and lively
Calling out or talking out of turn	Keen to contribute
Losing and forgetting things	Absorbed in own ideas
Distractible, impatient, daydreaming	Goal oriented; bored by mundane tasks: imaginative

Teaching strategy: ignoring minor upsets

Without her medication Mia has difficulty concentrating and in being still to listen. She is constantly bombarded by stimuli all vying for attention and so she constantly moves to answer the pull of something different out there. Understanding this, professionals try to ignore minor upsets so that her name is not always being called out. Affected children like Mia have a complex medical condition. They can appear as being disruptive because they lose patience and cannot wait to finish their work but this is outwith their control. They respond best to understanding within a calm environment. Strategies, e.g. having short tasks that can be finished and praised and being allowed to chill out when stress build up, really do make a difference. As children grow they can become more aware when tension is building and non-verbal children can sign that they need to be private or need physical activities to release their pent up emotion.

Sometimes the demands of calming the children can be eased by peers supporting the affected children. Many seem to be able to sympathise without speaking. In the classroom, peer help has been shown to benefit the 'buddy' as well as the needy child. The buddy can revisit learning activities in the guise of mentor. In her research into 'buddy programmes', Mastrangelo (2005) found that children with a learning difference and low self-esteem made the best buddy for children with ADHD because 'finally they could be cast as helpers rather than feel helpless'. In this way they were empowered!

Mia six months on

Mia has made real progress in the last six months. She has sustained cooperative play at tea parties and in tidying the playground. She is calmer for longer and this lets her listen and concentrate. She also shows her enjoyment, particularly in the gym. She wants to be first on the apparatus and is skilful in climbing and jumping and balancing – her confidence has grown so much. Some of the team have brought in make-up for her. She knows exactly where it is to go although the application is rather haphazard!

Mia goes happily to snack and lunch and eats well especially if there is 'marconi.' She asks for macaroni each time she sits at table. If this is not forthcoming she will try other foods. She is not in nappies but not totally reliable at the toilet either. She knows the hand washing routine now and will happily comply. She is coping and trying new words, e.g. 'Come on' to lead an adult to where she wants to go.

Planning

Mia enjoyed and sustained involvement in the Goldilocks story so the plan is to involve her in more simple stories with practical activities to back up the stories. 'The Three Little Pigs' and 'The Enormous Turnip' are possibilities.

It is fascinating that when some of the children are highly motivated they speak using difficult to articulate words. Callum's 'bubbles on' and Mia's 'Greg' and 'make-up' fascinated the team. They were anxious to discover more motivators!

The 'six months on' descriptions show how each young child is making progress through what are essentially play activities where the team have observed and made plans to develop the children's interests. But why is play so important as a learning medium for all children and perhaps especially so for children with complex needs? Chapter 2 explains.

The importance of play for enhancing learning for children with autism and other complex needs

A plea for time and understanding.

Please give me time to look and learn, to understand my day.
Please give me time to try things out before you show the way.
Please hold my hand and comfort me whenever things go wrong,
Please let me close my eyes awhile, the day can seem so long.
And please remember I am me and however much I try
I cannot do what others do,
Please teacher, tell me why?

                                        Christine Macintyre

This poem was written after finding that in many classrooms the pressure of time to get things done and meet curricular aims means that 'work things' take precedence over 'playtimes'. The poem tries to show the children's perspective on a day that can hold many joys but also many mysteries and frustrations. This is especially so if there is a constant implication that time is of the essence and certain skills must be acquired, i.e. that there is no time for play.

But why is play so important? Many professionals, after much time spent observing children, claim that it is not possible to define play. One teacher claimed 'it's like trying to catch the wind in a paper bag', and others have said that children do not differentiate between work and play; however, given the choice, many children, especially as they grow, would recognise the difference and choose play.

But if play is to be the cornerstone of the curriculum rather than 'only' a time for enjoyment, then a clear rationale including a list of possible benefits must be made.

So what is play?

As long ago as 1937, Susan Isaacs explained that, 'Play is a child's life and, through play, children come to understand the world around them'. And this definition has stood the test of time for it encapsulates the critical contribution to education that play makes. But can this be the same for children who learn differently, who have some kind of impediment that makes communication and understanding problematic? To answer this and justify play as the best means of providing education for all children, there must be an analysis that explains how every child can benefit from a curriculum based on play.

At play, the children can enjoy what they choose to do. They can decide on the tempo and the pace of the activity and are not stressed by someone else's expectations or by a plea to hurry. They can decide for themselves whether to continue playing or abandon what they are doing and begin something else with no fear of reprisal.

And with particular reference to children on the autistic spectrum, play skills are claimed to be strongly predictive of language development (Lewis 2003), and are thought to facilitate emotional and social development as well (Prelock 2006). In addition, Mastrangelo (2009a) has claimed a hugely important benefit. She writes, 'With extensive opportunities for play, the child's awareness of other people's mental states and intentions may be enhanced'.

This is very important as recognising that others have different thoughts and feelings is the basis for developing a ToM. So play houses a huge social and emotional potential for development.

Moreover, as they play, children's movement patterns are practised. Even in quite simple play scenarios, e.g. lining up bricks, fine motor skills such as the pincer grip are developed as they manipulate and sort objects. And if playing involves trundling a bike or jumping from a wall, then gross motor skills that involve balance, planning and decision-making (e.g. how far will I run? how fast will I go?) and self-awareness (e.g. am I confident enough to crawl through the caterpillar tunnel?) all enliven the children's repertoire of skills and enhance their self-esteem.

These aforementioned claims hold out hope for progress in all aspects of the children's development and particularly for developing the very areas that children with complex needs find most challenging, i.e. understanding the way other people think and how this influences the way they act.

In addition, children at play can develop their own scenarios or learn to share them with a friend. In this way their imaginations can blossom and hopefully they find satisfaction in creating something that is particularly their own.

But what about children who find it difficult to choose; to join with others in a play activity, to ask for support in finding resources, even finding something to play at? Can this be the best way for children with complex needs to learn?

For most children, play is an integral and pleasurable part of childhood, a time when typically developing children learn to integrate with others, to use various resources and tools and so practise their manipulative skills. They set and solve increasingly complex tasks and so develop their problem-solving abilities, their move-ment skills, their imaginations and self-awareness and hopefully through all of those experiences, a positive self-esteem. Gradually they are able to appreciate that others have different ideas and intentions from their own. But many children on the spec-trum are unable to appreciate what others are thinking or doing and so unable to understand or rationalise what others are playing at, and are often denied these natural learning opportunities. The essence of their condition makes pretending or imitating others less intuitive, so learning by copying is hard.

Furthermore if adults suggest, 'why don't you do that?', and the children comply, they lose the ownership of what is going on, so the question must be, 'is the activity still play?' If the child has become the follower rather than the instigator, if 'free choice' has been lost, surely the child who finds it difficult, even impossible to appreciate someone else's intentions must have less chance of understanding what is going on.

Wolfberg (2003) suggests that there are five necessary elements of play. These are:

- Play is enjoyable, freely chosen by the player
- Play has no preconceived outcome – the agenda can develop as play goes on
- Play can be abandoned without blame
- Play involves an element of make-believe
- Play often counteracts stress.

The second on the list is particularly apt for children who naturally see details rather than whole pictures. The children begin with a plethora of details and at that stage they do not know where they are going – the play scenario emerges and the details fuse into patterns that only they understand. If this 'works' then they can develop it, if not they can let it go and start again. This is why observing and waiting are the key function of those who aim to make their intervention pertinent or indeed to justify not intervening at all.

Thinking through these criteria, the question of pretending arises. Is it realistic to expect children on the spectrum to use 'make believe?' to pretend? This question stimulated others which formed the basis for discussion and action within the research. These were:

1) What did different children choose to play at and what kind of learning was implicit in each activity? (i.e. social, motor, intellectual or emotional)
2) Was it possible to discern how this activity might be linked to the activities of daily living? Could any opportunities to explain transfer be part of the teaching script? (i.e. how a competence developed in one venue could be used in another)
3) Did some children actively dislike time for play and could the team identify why?
4) Was constant repetition an issue?
5) Was there any evidence of simple or advanced pretend play?
6) What benefits did the child gain from time at play?
7) These questions structured the investigation through regaling different children's play experiences and studying and reporting how they impacted on the child.

The next case study is hugely revealing.

Case study for Leon

Meet four-year-old Leon now and celebrate the breakthrough made by his nursery nurse, Liz. Find how she facilitated his play by following a game he had initiated. But first meet Leon.

Leon is a four-year-old with corn coloured hair and big blue eyes. He is quite severely affected by autism. He usually prefers to be on his own, ignoring other children with no animosity, just a calm but determined withdrawal. He loves to get into the resources cupboard to sit on the floor, waiting for someone to come in. He is totally unfazed by the dark. His favourite activity is trying to crash the door of the cupboard or the classroom shut – a nightmare scenario for the staff team who have to be constantly alert in case a door is left ajar.

He is slightly built which is not surprising given his unwillingness to eat. His parents send in open sandwiches cut into six squares (he will eat these at home, but often are ignored at school) and they provide grape juice but this is often untouched, unless one of the other children discovers his special, rejected box! He is not interested in what the other children eat and doesn't want to sit at the table. Outdoors he runs around fairly aimlessly watching the others. However, one day after crouching and watching, he decided to get into one of the back seats on Kieran's bus! He didn't smile but his eyes seemed more alert. The fact that he joined in and sat close beside another child in the 'bus' was a big step forward. Did he understand? Was he pretending, was he pleased to be part of an activity or was he just so pleased to have a ride?

Now listen to Liz, an experienced nursery nurse, as she describes her 'breakthrough' with Leon. She explains:

> In the first few days of starting school, Leon seemed content although there was not much interaction between him and the staff or his peers. He was quite happy to do his own thing, which often meant he was opening and shutting doors, oblivious to requests or suggestions to play with toys.
>
> I put music on the tape recorder one morning at choosing time when Leon was sitting in a secluded spot nearby. He came over and switched the music off and he gave me some eye contact. Although this was very brief it was so important. On seeing this I wanted to make the most of the small interaction. Leon had made his way back to his seat but was watching me. I looked at him and smiled as I put the music back on. Leon got out of his chair and again switched off the music and again gave me brief eye contact.
>
> We played this game a few times more and I decided to try and extend the play. I folded my arms in the pretence of being peeved at Leon for turning the music off and as I did this I noticed a flicker of a smile on Leon's face. We did this a few times, then I introduced wiggling my index finger over to the button when I was turning the music back on. Leon by this time was quite clearly smiling and giving me more eye contact. We played this game for over twenty minutes with me introducing small adjustments to the game e.g. shaking my head, pretending to conduct the music. By this time Leon was giggling. He knew I was pretending and he recognised we were sharing a game.
>
> Leon went on to copy some of my gestures. It was such a lovely experience and at the end of the play session I had a friend.
>
> Leon initiated this game lots of times over the following few days and I really felt that the interactions between Leon and the members of staff had been started by this shared interaction.
>
> I feel it is really important to observe the children carefully and seize every opportunity to engage with them. This game was initiated by Leon and it was something he enjoyed doing. I feel it helped Leon to be able to interact with the members of staff and in doing so, build relationships. In the long run this helped Leon feel safe and secure in his new school.

What did Leon learn?

Social and emotional gains

This was a lovely example of developing the child's communication by following his lead. Importantly he recognised that Liz was pretending and he was able to empathise with Liz's pretended displeasure giving eye contact and giggling to show he was enjoying the play. These social and emotional gains were so pleasing. They hinted that Leon was just beginning to develop a Theory of Mind. This gave such a positive aura to Leon' progress. Liz's eyes were shining and his daily diary going home was overflowing with good cheer!

Intellectual gains

The turn taking that was established was an important precursor for development of conversations. Leon recognised the meaning behind different gestures and was happy to revisit the game.

Motor gains

The motor interaction was important too. Leon ran over to accomplish a task and then retreated to watch Liz's reaction. His 'switching off' had to be quick and precise. He used the pincer grip to great effect.

But how well did Leon's response meet the criteria for play? Although he did not initially generate the play idea, he latched on to the idea quickly and chose to keep the sequence going. His smiles and eye contact communicated sustained pleasure and his response to Liz's gesturing endorsed the idea that he was understanding her make believe. Would this lead him to develop his imagination or understand cause and effect? The interaction showed that Leon fully understood that Liz was pretending, he recognised that her gestures displayed a change in her emotions. Was he on the verge of pretending too?

It was important for the researchers to verify the change in Leon through continuing to observe in case this was a 'one-off' change.

Leon, six months on. Written by his nursery nurse Liz and teacher Jane

Reflecting on how much Leon has moved on in the last six months has made us so happy and proud of that little boy. Leon is now much more confident and trusting, enabling him to try new things. His eye contact has improved so much and we would say he actually seeks out interactions with staff and a couple of the children. Leon now uses PECS and although not really a spontaneous user will happily use his PECS in a structured setting. He takes part in the morning circle routine where children are welcomed one by one by the 'hello' song. And when the children choose a photo from a photo strip and give it to the pictured child (this is a strategy to help the children recognise the others in the class and learn their names) he readily joins in. Now he will sit with the others at snack and lunch although he will only eat a few crisps supplied by home. Sadly his sandwiches and yoghurt are still ignored.

Leon confidently moves around the school now and particularly enjoys going to gym where he excels. PE specialist Sam makes sure he is praised and he is beginning to look pleased. He is balanced and strong despite his poor appetite.

His picture, in the introduction, shows how well balanced Leon is. He is practising alone and content to be so. In class he is seeking out eye contact, sometimes holding the faces of the staff still and close for a moment or two to ensure this happens. He is almost toilet trained now which is a huge step forward. Everyone is pleased. He has learned to do so many things – the next step is encouraging him to eat and helping him to pretend.

The switch

When another teacher, Jake, heard of Leon's enjoyment and social progress after switching off the tape recorder, he immediately recalled a similar incident with another child which he also described as a breakthrough. He explained:

> When Rosa came to our school, she was ten and she was distressed and angry. It was very difficult for her to stay and to make any progress. She resisted any overtures, yet being alone didn't help her either. Then one day as we went in to the classroom I switched on the light. As she heard the click, she froze and immediately switched it off again. We repeated the on/off several times and she smiled and somehow that let her come into the classroom and into the group. I always wondered whether it was the noise or the shared action but I was sure that that event had made such a difference to the child.

Sutton-Smith (1997) offers one explanation. He claims that:

> Many children with autism spectrum disorder are actually engaging in play when they are immersed in what psychologists deem stereotypic or perseverative behaviours such as rocking, spinning wheels, flicking light switches, and so forth. These are forms of solitary play for the child with autism spectrum disorder because they provide escape or relaxation from a sometimes overwhelming environment of sights, sounds, smells, and tastes.

Sutton-Smith therefore expands the definition of behaviours that can legitimately be called play.

Are there other benefits to this activity, which is essentially copying what is seen?

Developing mirror neurons

Child of Our Time author Robert Winston (2004) cites Rizolatti and Fabi-Destro's (2009) claim that there are neurons, i.e. thinking cells, in the brain that are only activated when we watch another human carrying out a purposeful task. These he called 'mirror neurons.' He explains that, 'with knowledge of these neurons you have the basis for understanding a host of very enigmatic aspects of the human mind e.g. empathy, imitation learning, even the evolution of language'.

So Liz and Leon's exchange as well as that of Jake and Rosa could have important benefits through stimulating the formation of new neurological pathways in the children's brain. Certainly the observation that both children could copy and enjoy an extended exchange was very encouraging. But could play competences be developed further? Could they learn to pretend?

Key strategy: developing pretence

Leslie (1987) claims that 'autistic children cannot suspend their disbelief in propositions that have no literal truth in order to act in a pretend mode' and indeed observing children lining up bricks or spinning tops apparently oblivious to events in the environment around them, would appear to make this a viable hypothesis. She explains that this is not due to intellectual delay because other children of similar intellectual ability, e.g. those with Down's syndrome, have well developed pretence skills. It appears to be something particular to autism.

Many children with Down's syndrome are 'good players', perhaps due to the gene discovered by Arron (2006) that promotes socialisation especially in the early years. Hopefully this social gain may help counteract the intellectual difficulties that are part of that condition. It certainly reinforces the idea that children's understanding of the social world may be critical in stimulating pretend play experiences. In the early years especially, children with Down's syndrome are usually anxious to play and they appreciate any support in developing their ideas. Sadly, this sociability often wanes as the children grow and become more aware of their difficulties. At times they even work out self-defeating strategies that prevent them learning (or perhaps they prevent them failing?), so teachers should not be distracted by a cuddle and then find the lesson has been delayed! The problem-solving skills children employ can be surprising and subtle!

In relation to Leslie's claim that pretending is unlikely for children with autism, Hughes (1989) urges caution. He explains:

> It is conceivable that children with autism rarely produce pretend play, not because they completely lack the ability to do so, but because the kind of object-directed play they use can be carried out without pretence. A human drama, however, cannot be staged unless one can imagine the goals, perceptions, emotions and beliefs of the actors in the drama.

So what strategies can we use to help the children?

Strategies to develop pretend play

Greenspan and Wieder (1998) offer some advice:

- Introduce the child to symbolic play e.g. when the child wants juice, then make teddy thirsty too
- Identify some real life experiences the child knows and enjoys and have play props available to play out those experiences
- Encourage role-play with dressing up props and puppets
- Help the children elaborate on their intentions – ask e.g. 'who is driving the car? Where is it going? Does the driver have the keys?'
- Insert obstacles into the play e.g. make the bus block the road so that the children become involved in problem-solving. Through discovering different possibilities, they begin to recognise that other people have different ideas.

Figure 2.1 Cooking out of doors in the rain is fun!

Simple and advanced pretend play

There are two kinds of pretence that call on rather different understandings.

Simple pretend

In simple pretend, e.g. when a child pretends someone else is at the other end of their telephone or when children feed a doll or stir a pot in the kitchen or make a toy train run on rails or buy fruit in a pretend shop, they are pretending at the simple level. These scenarios are based on observation and action and do not require the child to consider intent, i.e. to appreciate what someone else is thinking or feeling.

Advanced pretend

In advanced pretend, the child must enter into the feelings of other people. Children must appreciate the mental state of another person. This is the basis of developing a ToM. So they must understand caring for someone who is hurt or helping someone carrying a heavy parcel or spontaneously show concern when another child's distress shows that something has caused disappointment or anger.

So, revisiting the episode where the children fed the bear, were they doing this as simple pretend, i.e. following the story where all three bears had bowls of porridge, or were the children imagining that the bear was feeling hungry and would feel satisfied after the meal? And afterwards, when some children stayed by the bear with the sore tummy to offer comfort, surely they were demonstrating advanced pretend?

Why is advanced pretend important?

If children are not able to engage in advanced pretend, then they would be unable to observe someone else's behaviour without appreciating the beliefs and intentions that had led to it happening. They would see an action but not fathom why it was happening. Not being able to interpret non-verbal behaviour would add to the confusion. It is claimed that non-verbal behaviour holds 90 per cent of the meaning in any communication so any deficit in interpreting this can be a main cause of isolation.

Strategy to develop advanced pretend

The team aimed to be more explicit in explaining why other people felt as they did and how they displayed that emotion. So instead of, 'Please hang your coat on the peg', they would elaborate the response 'I feel happy when you hang your coat up and that makes me smile'. They intended to overact in pretend scenarios and use strong eye contact when this was appropriate. This follows advice given by (Wieder and Greenspan 2003) when they write:

> During spontaneous floor-time play sessions, adults or children follow the child's lead by using affectively toned interactions, gestures, and words coupled with exaggerated affect to move the child up the symbolic ladder. The adult or child must establish a foundation of shared attention, engagement, simple and complex gestures, and problem-solving to usher the child into the world of ideas and abstract thinking.

Strategy: naughty teddy

Another idea was to have a 'naughty teddy' in class. Then, when he forgot to hang up his coat or spilt paint on the floor, the staff could explain, 'Teddy was silly today. He forgot that making a mess would make us all sad. Let's all look sad for a moment. What will we say to teddy now?' In this way good behaviour could be emphasised without 'blaming' any child. Such an explanation also stresses the dual effect of any behaviour, i.e. that actions have implications and that recipients can be harmed emotionally as well as in physical ways. Such a communication allows the staff to share 'being cross' with the child who then learns about good behaviour without being at fault. In this way the child's self-esteem is protected. With older children 'Mr Nobody' can replace teddy.

Considering the social dimension within play

As part of maturation, typically developing children pass through developmental sequences as they play, progressing naturally from sensorimotor play – where they learn about the properties of objects through mouthing or feeling – to solitary play that involves exploration and finding how things work. Thereafter, children become more aware of others and what their play involves and so they progress from parallel play (playing nearby but not integrating with another child) to pretend play where imagination and creativity allows them to devise ways of playing with others and joining in, even understanding the unwritten rules of a game.

Wolfberg (1999), concerned with children who have ASC, lists the social dimensions of their play as:

- Isolate play (playing alone)
- Orientation or observational play (watching others play)
- Parallel play (playing alongside one or more peers without interaction)
- Common focus play (engagement in a joint activity with one or more peers) and
- Common goal play (collaboration with one or more peers with an organised purpose).

For many children with ASC and other complex needs, however, these developmental sequences are very slow to emerge. The implicit difficulties of their condition (deficits in imitation, observing, and understanding emotion along with poor motor skills) mean that many children find it very difficult to initiate and sustain play even when they are alone. Of course, the degree of impairment varies from child to child and some social impairment may be situation dependent (Mastrangelo 2009a). This shows the importance of observers identifying competences in different environments and at different times of day so that different impacting variables, e.g. tiredness, are considered.

Strategy: setting the environment to develop socialisation

Macintyre and Leslie write:

- Play skills complement the development of motor skills – gross, fine and manipu-lative skills are all part of any play activity (Macintyre 2012) and
- Through play children can learn to understand and empathise with others so stimulating a ToM (Leslie 1987).

So how can professionals encourage children with ASC to learn to play and so move up through the hierarchy of play skills? If some children do not develop the skills naturally, should the adults not observe and follow the children, recognising where they are and find how they can follow them, always keeping the underlying necessary skills in mind?

Table 2.1 Some difficulties that cross 'labels' and make playing hard work

Intellectual difficulties	*Movement difficulties*
• Not knowing what to do • Not being able to follow the unwritten rules of someone's game, so not contributing appropriate ideas to take the play forward • Having a poor memory, so forgetting yesterday's play ideas • Having too many ideas but not being able to plan or organise play resources or ideas • Not understanding/being able to cope with changes in routine	• Not being able to balance on stepping stones or on a bike • Being clumsy and knocking into others • Being too active and out of control • Being uncoordinated, especially at the midline of the body, so spilling water, messing up puzzles • Being unable to grasp/release items • Being unable to throw or catch a ball • Body build difficulties, making children avoid movement practices
Social difficulties	*Emotional difficulties*
• Being unable to communicate effectively • Poor articulation, making interaction difficult • Being too timid to join in • Being reluctant to share or wait for a turn • Snatching rather than asking • Preferring to be alone – all the time • Only wanting what someone else has	• Being unable to understand pretending • Lack of imagination to develop play ideas • Poor concentration; little focus or staying power • Inability to understand what someone else is thinking or feeling, so responding inappropriately • Not responding at all • Completely immersed in own solitary play • Aggressive when thwarted • Poor empathy and altruism, so unable to understand other children's perspectives

The dichotomy between learning through play and a skills based approach

Whenever play is mentioned as a key learning tool, there is a dichotomy between adults who wish to give the children total freedom to choose their activity, to repeat their choices as often as they wish or to abandon what they have chosen to do with no fear of reprisal or even urging them to complete their task, and others who see learning as primarily a structured or directed experience with pre-set aims and outcomes. The first group believe that there is enough inherent learning within a freely chosen play endeavour to make it worthwhile particularly because they believe children will choose appropriately according to their developmental stage and so reveal and develop their interests naturally. They believe that careful observations can reveal hidden aspects of the children's development and behaviour and that this can lead to accurate recordings of the things children choose to do and things they avoid. This would lead to the production/selection of the most appropriate strategies for support. (See Chapter 6 for pie chart recordings.)

In contrast, McConnell (2002) and Barry *et al.* (2003) both claim that, 'Play skills and greeting skills improve best when they are specifically taught'. McConnell describes one kind of specific intervention as 'Social Skills Training (SST)' and advocates the teaching of 'maintaining eye contact and initiating conversations'. However, educationalists (e.g. Peter Dixon 2012 in his wonderful book of child-led activities, *Let me be*), afraid that adult intervention would result in young children losing ownership of their play to adults who perhaps had very different notions as to what the play was about, queried 'Are there social engineers on the swings?'

For both groups, however, observations would lead to setting aims in terms of motor, social, emotional and intellectual development. But which teaching process would be more successful? Would this depend on the age of the children or the level of their learning difference? Social aims for the more experienced children might include encouraging them to share their toys and to learn to care for someone else; in the younger groups they might be fulfilled by one child allowing another to sit nearby. Intellectual aims might be children learning to count and read and write their names; they might be remembering and identifying the characters in a story using laminated pictures and storyboards. For motor or movement development the children would be observed to find if activities had helped their balance to be improved or it could be that the children could now catch a ball or kick one into a goal.

And indeed the two sides of the equation rise again when we focus on play as a key learning tool for children on the autistic spectrum. Given their reliance on routine and structure, would having playtime as a key learning strategy dismantle what had been achieved in terms of the acquisition of skills or would it release the children to try 'activities deemed meaningful to them?' Would providing more resources stimulate the children to try new things and lead to setting higher aims? With the more severely affected children would this even be possible? How would they react to the freedom to make choices? In this research, where many of the children learn differently to neurotypical children, the team aim to have a balance of free play and more delineated opportunities and will evaluate each as the research progresses. Mastrangelo (2009a) succinctly sets out the differences. She explains,

> the various play approaches generate different results among children with autism spectrum disorders because of the variability among the children and because the focus may be either skill-based (i.e., to elicit eye contact with a peer) or more broadly based (i.e., to increase the number of spontaneous initiations during cooperative play). Given that children with autism spectrum disorder differ considerably in their cognitive and social abilities, there is a need to begin plotting which child characteristics seem to be more compatible with specific play approaches.

In so writing she defines the next strategy for the team, i.e. matching each child's inherent preference and ability to the way play is encouraged and structured.

A final word from the National Autistic Society:

> Following the child's lead rather than directing them will enable them to learn to communicate while they do things with another person, hence increasing their interaction. The child that leads is more likely to pay attention to the activity, more likely to focus on the same thing as the adult and will learn how to make choices for themselves.

autism.org.uk (2015)

N.B. At a meeting with parents, one mum explained that her daughter had been absorbed in pretend play when she was three and four. She had looked after her doll, feeding it and washing and generally showing care and concern. But by six, that had all disappeared and she showed no pretend play at all. This raises the issue as to whether there is a key time slot for developing pretend play, and if that is missed then is that kind of play hard, even impossible to retrieve? This is similar to the development of language and underlines the critical importance of the early years. More research is needed, for if children cannot pretend, what implications does this have for them developing a ToM?

The photocopiable resources that follow can be used to show the learning potential within play scenarios. They are subdivided into the four aspects of development so that activities to fit the children's general or specific needs can be highlighted and resources to develop play in that area can be provided. The analysis also shows potential ideas for transfer of learning from one scenario to another, thus aiding habituation.

Intellectual

Mother, father, baby, visitor, pet dog	Role-play
Fruit, seeds, nuts, sandwich fillings, pitta/brown bread	Choosing healthy foods for tea
Menus for lunch — where to buy vegetables/flour etc.	Discussing what to buy
Spoonfuls at baking time	One-to-one correspondence
Setting the table, matching, sorting	Counting
What different visitors, e.g. aliens, would like to eat	Imagining

Movement (motor)

Dressing and undressing	Doll/baby hanging up aprons, coats
Preparing food	Baking, chopping, washing, mixing, shredding, spreading, arranging on plates
'Ironing'	Flattening and folding tea cloths
'Writing'	Picture 'invitations' to the tea party

Learning in the house corner

Drinks, food and treats	Sharing
Choosing favourite foods for baby/visitor/alien	Caring
Passing plates, pouring juice	Taking turns
Waiting, saying 'thank you'	Being a helper; being a guest
Talking with all the people at tea	Communicating

Social

Appreciating	Taking responsibility Being 'in charge'
Gaining satisfaction	When 'guests' have a lovely time
Empathising	With guests who might be timid
Overcoming fears and worries	Trying new tasks — phobias reduced
Being able to stay near another person	Tolerating sitting beside a child

Emotional

from: *Enhancing Learning through Play*, Routledge © 2012 Christine Macintyre

Intellectual   **Movement (motor)**

Building a cave that   Learning about   Placing   Small world figures
won't collapse; or a   floating and sinking
paper boat that will float   Controlling   Water flow in
in the moat   Problem solving   filling/emptying tubes,
                                                                           syphons
Dry and wet sand —   Estimating levels;   Building   Wet sand; strengthening
selecting and adapting   pailfuls needed   hands, arms and shoulders

Of water/ice/freezing   Understanding   Developing coordination at the
melting disappearing   changing properties   midline of the body

Displacement of water when blocks
are added to the tray; submerging

Floating and sinking   Investigating

| **Learning at the water tray and sand tray** |

A day at the seaside   Discussing
                         Anticipating
A sandcastle with a moat Cooperating to
                         build a scene
                                                 Enjoying   The feel of water at different
                                                               temperatures
Splashing water   Looking out for
Scattering sand   others   Splashing, swirling, mixing colours

Ideas and equipment   Sharing   Making firm sandcastles

                                                 Creating   'Miniatures' of real events,
                                                               e.g diggers

                                                 Appreciating Ideas and developments

Social   **Emotional**

from: *Enhancing Learning through Play*, Routledge © 2012 Christine Macintyre

Intellectual

Vegetables/fruit/flowers

Recognising plants in the garden

Sizes of plants
Speed of growth

Comparing

Providing food — making fat balls, bird bath/table

Attracting birds and mini-beasts to the garden

Learning about poisonous plants/ deciduous plants

Safety in garden equipment

Safety issues

Keeping the garden tidy/ free from litter

Responsibility

Learning what fruits/veg will grow — and what dishes they will make, e.g that chips are cut-up potatoes!

Fruits
Vegetables

Movement (motor)

Planting

Bulbs and following their growing cycle

Watering

Carrying a watering can

Pouring

The water gently so as not to disturb plants

Stepping

Gently to avoid damaging the plants

Controlling

Scattering seeds carefully

Covering

Delicate plants with fleece in the winter

Learning in the garden area

Collecting conkers to see the prickles (to keep the seed secure)

Collecting seeds together in the autumn

Appreciating

How beautiful plants are; how delicate plants are

Watching

The process of seeds maturing and growing

Preparing a patch of soil

Working together

Plants and seeds for tubs

Choosing/discussing

Tending

Watering, feeding, supporting plants

Taking care of a plot together

Having responsibility in twos or threes

Observing

Slow growth — delayed gratification

Social

Emotional

from: *Enhancing Learning through Play*, Routledge © 2012 Christine Macintyre

Intellectual

Rhythm — Learning

Different qualities of sound — Accompanying

Different instruments — Recognising

The beats — Counting

The different instruments — Naming

Words of songs — Planning

The number of instruments — Organising

Movement (motor)

Playing — Different instruments

Controlling — Sounds

Coordinating — Two hands doing different things

Two hands doing the same things (cymbals)

Controlling — Length of sound

Accompanying a dancer

Learning in the music corner

Appreciating — Tone

Playing together — Cooperating

Understanding — (a) That black notes are symbols for sounds

(b) How sounds can represent ideas, e.g. fire crackling, rain pattering

Basic compositions — Sharing

To others making sounds — Listening

Investigating — Different sounds and how they can make sound story

For instruments — Caring

Within the group about the sounds — Talking

Responding — To sounds

Gaining confidence — In playing and listening

Social

Emotional

from: *Enhancing Learning through Play*, Routledge © 2012 Christine Macintyre

Intellectual

The sequence of actions — Planning

Equipment and resources — Organising

Remembering what comes first then next — Sequencing

Completing the action — Doing

Estimating distances/heights — Judging

Knowing when to jump, throw, chase etc. — Timing

Movement (motor)

Balancing — On benches before and after jumping

Coordinating actions, control — Slowing down and stopping at the correct time

Transitions — Joining two actions together

Gross motor skills — Crawling, climbing, walking, running, jumping, rolling*

*pencil rolls only for children with Down's syndrome

Outdoor play on large apparatus

Social

Learning to let others go first (developing understanding of how others feel) — Waiting, Taking turns

Watching others; copying good ideas on seesaw — Cooperating

Ball skills, e.g. throwing/catching/aiming — Being part of a team

Matching movements; fitting in spaces — Making up a movement game in twos

Emotional

Paying attention — Remembering and carrying out instructions

Gaining confidence — Becoming motivated to try more movement sequences

Endorphins working

Releasing tension/energy/stress — Running, jumping, wheeling

Reducing cortisol — Calming down

from: *Enhancing Learning through Play*, Routledge © 2012 Christine Macintyre

Chapter 3

Theoretical underpinnings for the first selection of strategies

This chapter explains some theoretical underpinnings for the first selection of strategies and offers more linked ideas to try. These are,

- Sensory perception and integration
- Pointing as communication
- Crawling using the cross lateral pattern
- Reflexes and their influence on learning.

Sensory perception and integration

Grandin (2014) highlights the vital importance of monitoring children's sensory perception. She writes:

> Sensory disorders are not just an autism problem. Studies of non-autistic children have shown that more than half have a sensory symptom; that one in six has a sensory problem significant enough to affect his daily life and one in twenty should be diagnosed with a sensory processing disorder.

She bemoans the lack of research in this area, hypothesizing that to gather data, 'researchers would need to look at the world through an autistic person's jumble of neuron misfires'.

Difficult indeed, but the topic is critically important if many, even most children with learning disabilities/autism have some sensory impairment. Perhaps they hear too much and become overwhelmed by noises or too little so that they miss conversations or learning cues, or they may have poor auditory discrimination that prevents the accurate hearing of subtle sounds or even causes them to miss the first letter of a word. They may be tactile hypersensitive so that even slight nudges are painful so they avoid people and places that might cause hurt, or in contrast they may be hyposensitive and not feel pain or extremes of cold or heat at all. This sounds alright until illnesses or accidents happen and no one is aware. Some children see too much detail in presented material and in the environment around them and find selection and focus difficult, while others have poor vision and don't see enough. Some children cannot bear to touch clay or get their hands dirty, others find balancing difficult and concentrating on keeping upright and steady detracts from relaxed learning. It is not difficult to understand why these children are stressed. No wonder Carter (2000) claims that children's sensory input has a huge impact on their capacity to learn. This is because, 'the brain does not "see", "hear", or "feel" the outside world; it constructs responses to stimuli from the senses'.

In similar vein, Sally Goddard (2002) describes the process of learning. She writes:

> All learning takes place in the brain, but it is the body which acts as the vehicle by which knowledge is acquired. Both brain and body work together through the central nervous system and both are dependent on the senses for all information about the outside world.

The sensory system is part of the nervous system. For efficient and accurate learning all parts of the process must be intact and function harmoniously.

If decreased or inaccurate sensorimotor experiences impair neurobehavioral function, however, then one might expect that increasing sensorimotor stimulation would enhance it. In fact, 'enriched sensorimotor experiences reliably enhance dendritic branching, synaptic density, and neurogenesis' (van Praag *et al.* 2000) and this burgeoning of neural connections in the brain means that new skill development is possible (Woo and Leon 2013).

The sensory receptors take information from the external environment through seeing, hearing and feeling (i.e. through the visual, auditory and tactile senses and those of taste and smell) and through the internal ones (i.e. the vestibular, proprioceptive and kinaesthetic senses).

Sensory acuity is so vital for learning that each one has been explained below.

The vestibular sense

The vestibular sense, which controls balance, is critically important because all other senses pass through the vestibular mechanism at brain stem level. This means that

Table 3.1 The senses with indicators of difficulties

The senses	Their key role	Indicators of difficulties
Vestibular	Balance, coordination and control	Unsteadiness; unwilling to leave the ground or take risks
Kinaesthetic	Spatial awareness	Unable to judge distances; bumping and spilling
Proprioceptive	Body awareness	General clumsiness; falling over thin air and being hurt
Visual	Seeing and tracking	Squinting; rubbing eyes; holding a book too near or far from the face
Auditory	Listening and hearing	Distractibility; strange responses. Poor differentiation of sounds
Tactile	Feeling and touching	Needs firm touch or can't bear to be touched. Difficulties with personal space
Taste and smell	Tells about preferred foods; indicates pleasant and unpleasant events	Unwilling to try foods or go into new environments where 'smells' offend

input from all the other senses must be matched to the vestibular before their information can be processed. The vestibular is the first sense to 'work' and even in the womb it is important in getting the baby in the head down position ready to be born. Babies who have a breech birth MAY go on to have dyspraxia, i.e. a difficulty in planning and carrying out movements efficiently. This happens because their sense of balance was not working properly before birth. From then on the vestibular sense controls any change in posture or alignment – it is part of everything we do, either as dynamic or moving balance or static balance that keeps the body steady in stillness. It even helps the acquisition of hand and foot dominance that is important in controlling a pencil to write and draw and contributes to all forms of movement patterning. Not having a dominant hand or foot can cause confusion, fluffing the action and cause delay in responding. Balance is very important. It 'is vital for posture, movement and it contributes to a developing sense of self' (Bee and Boyd 2005) and so affects the self-esteem. And as all other sensory input passes through the balance mechanism en route to analysis in the higher centres of the brain, an underdeveloped vestibular sense can hinder all aspects of learning.

Children with a poorly developed vestibular sense would be likely to:

- Look uncontrolled, falling over and getting hurt
- Suffer from motion sickness or giddiness
- Dislike quick changes of direction
- Avoid funfairs or playgrounds with swings
- Be easily disoriented and flustered
- Be clumsy, dropping things
- Have great difficulty in standing or sitting still
- Misjudge distances, e.g. in jumping down or stopping at the kerb.

Strategies to help

The vestibular system could be compared to having an internal compass that tells us about directions, e.g. forward, up, down and sideways. It allows the body to change direction in a controlled manner. Balance demands increase as the support base diminishes. So, in teaching activities, begin with a wide base, e.g. ask the children to:

a) Lie on the floor or on the grass, roll over and roll back keeping the body long and straight.
b) Still in lying, ask 'Without looking, can you feel your toes? Wiggle them to show me where they are. Now, point them up into the air. Make your legs open wide and clap them together again'.
c) 'Make them cycle – slowly then very fast!'

To do this the balance base reduces gradually and through 'pushing into the ground', awareness of the back is enhanced.

d) In sitting, facing a partner, legs stretched out in front, sweep them open and closed. In twos, roll a ball into the space and trap it.
e) Still in sitting, bend up your knees and make thunder noises with your feet.

f)   In standing, stretch up high, clap your hands above your head. Stamp your feet at the same time. Move forward doing this then turn round in a circle. Staff should demonstrate and accompany the children!

Sing,

> Let's go children, follow me (marching forward)
> Wave the branches of your tree (this arm action is a balance challenge)
> When the wind blows loud and long (make the branches swoop up and down)
> Turn around and sing a song!

Any simple activity to help balance is beneficial. In the old days, 'sitting up straight' and 'walking tall' may have been good things to do!

The kinaesthetic and proprioceptive senses

These two names are often used interchangeably, however, to be accurate, the kinaesthetic sense only comes into play when there is muscle contraction, i.e. when the body is moving. The proprioceptive sense works all the time relaying positional information when the body is moving or at rest. The proprioceptors are located all over the body and in the muscles and joints. They literally tell us where we end and the outside world begins, so they stimulate a sense of 'body boundary'.

Interestingly, children with a poor proprioceptive sense often have difficulty being still – they have to move so that their kinaesthetic and proprioceptive senses working together provide them with more information about where they are in space. Their restlessness can be assuaged by being allowed to sit on a beanbag which allows some shifting of position. Some children need to hold something to stroke to help them listen.

Difficulties/observation points indicating a poor kinaesthetic or proprioceptive sense. The child is or has:

- A poor sense of poise, e.g. the child who tends to slump over the table (make sure the feet are supported, not dangling – on the floor and that the table is the correct height)
- Easily tired by the constant effort needed to stay erect
- Constant movement and fidgeting
- Poor depth perception causing stumbling or 'falling over thin air'
- Poor sense of direction (rehearse 'where to go' ahead of the child having to do so independently)
- Poor body awareness (play 'Simon says' types of games).

Ideas to stimulate proprioception

1)   Use rhymes that use rubbing the limbs, e.g. 'Rub a dub dub, three men in a tub'. Or,

'Today it is icy,
Just look at my nose,
It's all red and shiny and everyone knows,
It's Jack Frost that's been out,
to make us all chill,
But rub it and rub it!
He won't make us ill'
(From *Jingle Time*).

Figure 3.1 Michael doesn't feel where his feet are. This could be dangerous, e.g. in stopping at the kerb. Have fun tying a beanbag to his feet (with other children too) for the added weight helps awareness. Once they are happy to try this, they can try to take giant steps – a real balance challenge. Perhaps link this with the 'Jack and the Beanstalk' story or 'The Friendly Giant' story from *Jingle Time*.

2) Rub arms to get them warm, then stamp feet at the same time.
3) Bring rubbing into stories, e.g. 'Poor Sam has bumped his leg. We have to rub it to get it better – rub and rub. Can you rub your leg just like that?'
4) Stand with your back against the wall bars. Lean into the wall. Slowly slide down to sit, swivel round and pull up again.
5) Have a spinning cone and note if children can keep compact.

The visual sense

Assessing vision should cover much more than measuring near and distance vision that is often the main concern in a simple eye test. Children who 'pass' this can still have difficulties with tracking, i.e. following the words on a page, the writing on the board or catching a ball coming towards them. Functional vision depends on maturation of the central nervous system. Visual-motor integration skills are as important as distance sight. The two eyes have to work together to focus on an image (convergence).

Strategies

Some children with poor convergence will see double images that confuse letter recognition; others will see the letters move on the page and may endure severe eyestrain trying to adjust to the movement. This is now called visual stress – previously known as Mears-Irlen syndrome after the ladies who discovered it – and can be helped by coloured overlays or coloured lenses in spectacles. These have to be advised by an optician. Children also benefit from being allowed to choose the colour of paper that suits them for writing and drawing, as different colours defeat the reflection of light that can irritate the eyes and put children off their work. Reading can also be helped by having books with non-justified print. (Barrington Stoke, Publishers, Edinburgh supply books like this).

Children must also be able to adjust their focus so that they can decipher objects and print from different angles and directions. This is called accommodation. The three skills, convergence, accommodation and tracking are all prerequisites for quick identification and reading without strain.

Difficulties/observation points indicating a poor visual sense:

- Rubbing eyes or partially closing them to keep out the light
- Distress/loss of interest when books appear
- Difficulty following written work on the board
- Handwriting sloping in different directions
- Poor letter formation
- Moving a book around to catch the words.

The auditory sense

During the first three years, the child is listening and learning to tune in to sounds of his mother tongue and thereafter it is harder to adjust to the tenor of another language. This is one vital reason why specialist nurseries for children with learning delay should be provided. Obviously, loss of hearing significantly affects learning, but children who 'can hear' may have auditory discrimination problems and these may be a key impairment in a number of additional learning needs conditions e.g. dyslexia, dyspraxia, Down's syndrome. If the child cannot hear the difference between 'p' and 'b' or 'sh' and 'th' then both reading and spelling are impaired. Even silent reading is affected because then the child listens to an inner voice – if the sounds are not clear then this process will be affected just the same as in reading aloud.

Hearing too much (i.e. auditory hypersensitivity) can cause as much difficulty as not hearing enough. Children bombarded by sound can have difficulty selecting what they need to hear from the variety of different noises around them. Even in a quiet classroom, some children find hearing the teacher difficult, as they cannot cut out what to others would be minor rustles and squeaks.

Sounds are transmitted to the language-processing centre in the brain. The right ear is usually the more efficient because sounds heard there pass directly to the main language centre in the left hemisphere of the brain. In contrast, left-eared children have to pass the sound to the language sub centre and then through the corpus callosum to the left hemisphere for decoding. This slight delay may put left-eared children at a disadvantage.

Difficulties/observation points indicating a poor auditory sense. The children have or are:

- Easily distracted
- Over-sensitive to sounds
- A poor sense of pitch and tone
- Confusion in distinguishing letters
- Delay in responding
- Not hearing questions clearly, affecting responses
- Constantly asking for things to be repeated
- Ignoring instructions because they have not been heard.

(One parent was cross because her child reported, 'No school tomorrow, the teachers are all going boating'. It was election time!)

The tactile sense

Tactility or sensitivity to touch is important in feeding, in communicating and in generally feeling secure. Touch is one of the earliest sources of learning and touch receptors cover the whole body. They are linked to a headband in the brain called the somatosensory cortex. This registers heat, cold, pressure, pain and body position and makes an important contribution to the sense of balance.

Some children have a system that is over-reactive to touch and this causes them to withdraw or be distressed by hugs or even people approaching – responses that most children welcome. This can make them seem haughty and they become isolated. Sadly, peers can mistakenly interpret their reactions as snubs. Yet these same children can be 'touchers' seeking out sensory stimulation through contacting others even although they themselves would be distressed by such overtures. They don't appreciate the boundaries of personal space.

The pain receptors can cause difficulties too. Some children are hypo-sensitive and may not feel pain or temperature change – they may have a huge tolerance to holding hot plates or going out-of-doors ill clad in icy winds. And the hyper sensitive ones will over-react about injections and visits to the dentist. Some even feel pain when having their nails or hair cut and some cannot tolerate seams in socks or certain textiles in clothing. All kinds of problems arise from being hypo or hyper touch-sensitive.

Difficulties/observation points indicating a poor tactile sense. The children:

- Dislike being touched so withdraw from contact
- May be compulsive touchers
- May not register pain appropriately causing over or under reaction
- Have poor temperature control
- Are prone to stress and allergies – possibly eczema
- Dislike contact sports and games.

Strategies to make children aware of the effect of touching: developing hand awareness

a) Have some coloured ice in the water tray or sink. The children can make the water swirl as it melts.
b) Pop bubble paper.

c) Pick up dry macaroni to thread and colour.
d) Catch a balloon in a balloon bag without making it pop!

The senses of smell and touch

The sense of smell is the most evocative of the senses as it can stimulate memories, e.g. of a garden visited long ago or a hot summer when the milk turned sour! The sense of smell can also stimulate the hormones controlling appetite, temperature and sexuality. Certain smells can become associated with different situations, e.g. the smell of a hospital can conjure up memories of pain; the scent of flowers can recall a happy event such as a wedding or a sad one such as a funeral. These senses are controlled by the thalamus.

The sense of taste depends on the sense of smell so it is not difficult to understand why children often refuse to accept new foods because they do not like the appearance or the smell. Some of the earliest learning comes through these senses, as during the sensory motor period the baby will put everything to the mouth. This most sensitive part of the body will tell about the taste and the texture of the object and whether it is hard, soft or malleable as well as whether the taste is pleasant or not!

Difficulties/observation points indicating a poor sense of taste and smell

- Children may be very faddy about new foods and only tolerate a very restricted diet
- They may refuse to go to the bathroom because of the smell of antiseptics or even of scented soap
- They may dislike being near other people especially if perfume or after-shave is used
- They may be upset by floor polishes and other chemical sprays.

Sensory integration

Although the senses can be studied separately, they do support each other by working together. More and more with the research into dyslexia, it can be claimed that we 'read with our ears' (Peer 2004). A poor sense of smell also inhibits the ability to discriminate different tastes. This is the basis of sensory integration, e.g. hearing the approaching bus lets passengers judge the speed and allows them to prepare to board even before they see it. However, the balance needed to alight smoothly without stumbling (i.e. dynamic balance), can be affected if the visual sense does not complement the vestibular one. This is why sensory integration is often called cross-modal transfer. Reactions may vary according to the type of stimulus, its intensity, its rate and its duration. Most people can only tolerate a shrill sound such as a fire alarm or an intensive light for a short time without distress and sensory deprivation has been used as a form of torture leading to insanity.

These senses are stimulated by sensory receptors. Most of them are exquisitely sensitive to their specific energy form so they are clear as to their remit (e.g. the skin is not sensitive to normal light but is sensitive to touch), but usually several receptors/ senses work together. There are three main types.

Table 3.2

Sensory receptors	Sensitivity to
Mechanoreceptors	Mechanical stimuli such as pressure or stretch. Responsible for muscular tension
Thermoreceptors	Coldness and warmth
Chemoreceptors	Different smells and tastes

Some children are hyper (over) sensitive to some or all stimuli while other are hypo (under) sensitive and this affects their response time, their motivation, their compliance or comfort in different situations. Hypersensitive children can become overwhelmed by the inrush of stimuli to the extent that they have physical symptoms, e.g. abdominal pain or 'a closed throat' that prevents them reacting or responding. This withdrawal may only be released by the child moving to a more relaxing situation or by the child giving an aggressive response.

Some children, e.g. those with ASCs can acknowledge a stimulus without necessarily perceiving what is meant. They might see a road accident and only relate – on prompting – that there were fire engines and flashing lights. They might not empathize with the hurt people at all.

Pointing as communication

In the first case study with Callum, his nursery nurse Ellie set out to reinforce his pointing skills by ensuring that he was rewarded by having instant attention and a piece of banana (his chosen treat) when he did so. These gestures were important so that a shared experience could occur even in the absence of speech. A second outcome beyond building a relationship however, was claimed by Casenhiser *et al.* in 2013. They wrote, 'The child's ability to engage in and initiate joint attentional frames should be fostered as this predicts language development'.

Charman (2003) also explained that joint-attention abilities play a crucial role in development. They are associated with language gains and (less so) social and communication competences. Such claims gave extra credence to Ellie's choice of strategy for Callum.

Children with autism always display deficits in social interaction, usually showing little motivation to interact with others. These are a major source of impairment regardless of cognition or language ability – and these deficits do not remit with development (McConnell 2002). In fact they may increase as their social environment becomes more complex. The deficits also lead to anxiety and stress, hampering interaction further.

Barrett *et al.* (2004) in *Children on the Borderlands of Autism* offer some pointers for observation.

Table 3.3

Social behaviours	Observe and assess: does the child:
Social interaction	Hold eye contact?
Initiate	Gesture to obtain attention to self or to initiate interaction?
Social-interaction	Take part in interactive activities and games?
Respond	Respond to others in turn-taking games?
Joint attention initiate	Point out something or show and share a book or toy?
Joint attention respond	Follow directions e.g. 'LOOK!'
Imaginative domain	
Functional Play	Use objects conventionally, e.g. brush doll's hair?
Pretend Play	Refer to something not present?
	Use one thing as another, e.g. a yo-yo as a toy dog?

Many interventions teach specific skills, e.g. pointing and initiating interaction (Kasari *et al.* 2010). But Prizant *et al.* (2000) seek to teach children the functional skills consistent with play advice. Like Goddard-Blythe (2005), they suggest taking the child through the earlier developmental stages to 'give the brain a second chance'. Following their lead, Ingersoll *et al.* (2003) offer a list that would seem to complement a play-based approach.

Ingersoll's list

1) The adult joins the child's focus of interest
2) The adult arranges the environment to encourage initiations from the child
3) Communicative attempts are responded to as if they were purposeful, and
4) Emotional expression and affect sharing are emphasised.

Ingersoll named this Developmental Social Pragmatic interventions (DSP).

The ability to initiate contact means that more social interchanges can happen and this can gradually be built up through duos and eventually peer groups can be encouraged to sustain the communication. This in turn might lead to more natural turn taking, so encouraging interaction and language development. Rutherford *et al.* (2007) showed that joint-attention ability significantly predicts the ability to join in pretend play.

Lack of pointing skills can be an early indicator that something is amiss. Listen to Charlotte Moore (2012) describing how neither of her two sons, severely affected by autism, ever pointed to draw her attention to what was happening. She explained, 'They didn't realise that I couldn't know what was going on if I wasn't there – they thought I understood everything and so there was no need to point it out!'

She realised her third son was not autistic when he came to fetch her to help him retrieve a biscuit that had dropped into a watering can in the garden. 'He knew I couldn't know because I was not there! He understood that he needed to point it out! From that one shared experience, I knew he was not autistic.'

Pointing skills also develop awareness of gesture, i.e. non-verbal ways of requesting, of welcoming and rejecting people and things. Ninety per cent of meaning comes from non-verbal communications and although children with ASCs are less likely to search for meaning in an exchange, observers may be able to interpret their gestures and so meet their needs. Pointing is a very effective means of gaining attention. As a child, did you ever stand and point at the sky and find that other people around you gazed skywards too?

As a gesture, pointing is not as straightforward as it sounds. One father had taught his son, who was autistic, that helping himself to biscuits was not acceptable. If he pointed to the biscuit jar, then his father would come and help him have one. This worked well until one day his father saw him in an empty room, pointing and pointing to the biscuit jar and becoming angry and frustrated when there was no response. *The boy had not realised that the essence of pointing was to put an idea into someone else's mind. He could not understand that his quest needed another person.* There is also the 'old-fashioned(?)' advice that 'pointing is rude', in that it conveys some ridicule to the recipient and the gesture may warrant some unlooked for and unwelcome retaliation. How does one explain to a child with an ASC that there are times when, having learned to point, it might not be the best skill to use? How complicated it is!

Crawling using the cross lateral pattern

Crawling using the cross lateral pattern is so important because it provides:

1) A strengthening effect on muscles in the arms and legs, the neck and the trunk.
2) A balance practice in the safe table position (not far from the ground if toppling over occurs).
3) An early form of locomotion, so opening up avenues of exploration for the child.
4) Practice that develops visual acuity because the eyes follow the hands as they move.
5) Reduction in the effect of any retained primitive reflex that inhibits crossing the midline activities, e.g. combing the hair, using a knife and fork, turning pages in a book.
6) A definite link to writing competence and – at this time – a more tenuous link to reading.

N.B. The cross lateral pattern means that the hand on one side and the knee on the other go forward in sequence. Crawling using a homolateral pattern i.e. the hand and knee on the same side going forward together does not have the same benefits. Many adults who had difficulty with writing at school find they still cannot crawl using the CL pattern.

N.B. Staff should get down and try the action themselves to ensure they know how to teach it! Once one pattern is established, it can be difficult to change but, due to the implicit gains listed above, it is very worthwhile persevering.

Observation can be tricky when the children crawl quickly – if this is the case, ask them to crawl upstairs or climb on a climbing frame. This slows the pattern. Crawling can be built into a game – through tunnels, up stairs, round table legs. It is so important that children try.

But what happens if the children cannot adopt this pattern?

There is an age-related sequence of development prior to achieving the crawling action itself. This would help adults to spot where the children were in developmental

Figure 3.2 It is often easier to observe the cross lateral pattern as children crawl up stairs or use a climbing frame.

terms and when there was a difficulty or a reluctance to try, it would give them an indication of what preliminary stages could be helpful. Three- and four-year-olds enjoy showing you if they can roll over – they don't need to know it is a 'test!'

Table 3.4 An age-related developmental sequence (neurotypical) leading to crawling. The same sequence applies although the timing will be very different when children do not go through the sequence naturally as part of maturation.

20 weeks	Babies can roll over from lying on their backs to their fronts (supine to prone lying). They rotate their upper body then twist a leg over. This is a natural preparation for crawling.
28 weeks	Babies can roll over and push up supporting the weight of the upper body by the arms. The trunk is still low.
32 weeks	Movement forward begins but this is usually a pulling forward on the arms action with the trunk still low.
36 weeks	Gradually a raised crawling position is achieved – often a rocking action – hands and feet with bottom in the air is practised and this is important in eliminating the Asymmetric Tonic Neck Reflex (ATNR).
44 weeks	Progress – locomotion on hands and knees happens.

N.B. Unless there is a difficulty, children will go through this sequence of events when they are ready, when they have the strength and the neurological maturation to allow this to happen. It is an innate progression, down to nature rather than nurture. Some children will be skilled crawlers at seven months, others will wait till they are 17 months and both are fine. And many will take themselves through this sequence with no prompting or teaching needed. But if there is delay or a reluctance to adopt the cross lateral pattern, then knowing the sequence can prevent adults stressing the children by asking them to progress too quickly through the sequence.

From their earliest days, children should have plenty of tummy time. This encourages pushing up to see and strengthens the neck arms and shoulders muscles. The child will gradually attempt to pull along the floor showing progress is being made. Reluctant to move children may be encouraged by asking them to stretch one arm out for a toy but adults should not hurry the children unnecessarily. They will make progress when they have the strength and the neurological competence to do so. Children have an inbuilt motivation to move. Sometimes adults must just wait. Allied to that of course, are the number of opportunities babies are given. If they sit in a buggy all day, then practice sessions are missed. Once professionals in settings understand the implications of this, I hope they will share them with the parents and/or carers and that both will give the children many opportunities to crawl.

Strategies to develop the pattern

1) With the child in the table position, stand in front and dangle a toy so that the head is raised. Check that the child can retain the table position and does not flop back. Attaining and holding the table position shows that the child's vestibular sense or sense of balance is working well. Some children will not enjoy being on their fronts at the start. If they don't immediately take to this gentle encouragement – perhaps another child alongside – or mum or dad– can encourage them. Just keep the activity short and gradually increase the time as the child gains confidence. It is really worthwhile persevering.
2) With the child in a table position, play a game 'rocking from toes to hands' as children at the earlier stage of learning to crawl do. This action can help to inhibit a retained reflex. It also develops the idea of moving forward.
3) Take crawling back through the stages in the table. Learning to crawl using the cross lateral pattern gives the brain a second chance to make connections and achieve the most useful neuronal pathways.

Other social and intellectual benefits

Crawling also promotes social and emotional gains. The social one comes when the child crawls to meet or join in a game with another person and the emotional one comes from the achievement that probably merits praise, and the 'feeling of being-able-to-do' that enhances self-confidence and the self-esteem.

Body awareness

Children have to know where the different body parts are before efficient movement can happen. If they don't 'feel' where their feet are, how can they walk efficiently and if their fingers lack feeling, how can they use the pincer grip, i.e. the tripod finger grip necessary for precision and control? What can help?

Strategies to support body awareness which is part of the self-concept, i.e. the picture children develop of themselves as they grow:

> For the younger ones, extend the ideas in the favourite (extended) rhyme 'Head, shoulders, knees and toes' to bring in other body parts. The rhyme below shows how. The well-known first verse usually comes twice.

> Heads, shoulders, knees and toes, knees and toes,
> Heads, shoulders, knees and toes, knees and toes,
> Eyes and ears and chin and nose,
> Heads, shoulders, knees and toes.

> Heads, shoulders, knees and toes, knees and toes,
> Heels, bottoms, backs and nose, backs and nose,
> Tap your shoulders, turn right round,
> Stretch to the sky – don't make a sound.

> Make your fingers stretch out wide, stretch out wide.
> Now clap your hands against your side, against your side.
> Stretch arms out, make them whirl you round and round. Then
> Sit very quietly on the ground, on the ground.

Analysis of the extended version

In verse 2, the tapping comes up the back of the body rather than going down the front. This makes children aware of these parts of their bodies. Few activities ask children to be aware of their backs and as they can't see their backs this body part gets ignored. Can you think of any activities or songs that you use that refer to backs?

Then, the 'tap your shoulders' line asks the children to cross their hands in front to tap their opposite shoulder. This, apart from promoting shoulder awareness shows observers whether they can cross the midline of the body. Some children find this very difficult – it is as if there is a wall there. This could be part of a retained reflex and should be noted and expert help requested if the difficulty persists. If you are in doubt, ask the children to paint wide rainbows in the sky and see if they change hands at the apex of the arc.

This idea of 'crossing' can be expanded to tap the knees (in front and behind), the elbows and the ankles and once these games have been played and the children have learned all about the different body parts, the 'Simon says' games make a natural and useful progression.

In verse 3, stretching to the side develops spatial awareness and this contrasts with the hand and arm actions that 'clap against the side'. Stretching out and holding that position can be a difficult balance challenge so it's best to keep the rhythm brisk. The clapping against the sides provides a fun release and helps develop body awareness of where the sides are in relation to other body parts.

So in a simple game we have introduced the heels, the shoulders, the back and the sides, the elbows, the ankles and the back of the knees. That's good, because we don't talk much about these parts, do we?

My recommendation would be that jingles and crawling practices happened every single day. (For ideas about linking jingles with stories and poems see Macintyre (2003.) Challenges can be made by having children crawling over and under and through obstacles round table legs and up stairs. This keeps the play challenging and fun.

Activity for staff and children: in twos teach a colleague to crawl. It's fun!

a) First, carefully observe your partner crawling freely, but quite slowly over the room. Do not give any instructions, just watch.
b) If your partner uses the cross lateral pattern effortlessly, i.e. one hand and the opposite knee forward, change over and you try.
c) If your partner instinctively crawls using the homo lateral pattern, suggest s/he changes and watch to see how difficult adopting the cross lateral pattern is.
d) If the homo lateral pattern is the natural one, ask about any writing difficulties, for this is a key link. Ask about the birth; was it c-section or a breech birth? Was bum shuffling the preferred method of getting around?
e) In the crawling position, i.e. holding a flat table, ask your partner to stretch out one leg or arm – or both at the same time. Is balancing an issue?
f) Above all, check that the children in your setting can crawl using the cross lateral pattern. Especially if they have difficulties, play crawling games every day, no matter how old the children are. Handball is a popular and beneficial choice. It is never too late to help!

Reflexes and their influence on learning

When children have learning difficulties, their teachers must try to understand how retained primitive reflexes may be preventing their progress. There are a number of primitive reflexes present in every child, reflexes that have specific jobs to do and when these are accomplished, they should be replaced by more sophisticated postural reflexes that allow more challenging movements to be carried out with more control. This process is called inhibition. Observing the children can highlight if retained primitive reflexes are impacting on individual development.

The primitive reflexes should be inhibited in a specific sequence. They should not be active beyond 6–12 months of life. Their inhibition will coincide with the emergence of a new skill. This is why the presence or absence of these reflexes at certain times can be used as assessments of the maturity of the central nervous system (CNS). If primitive reflexes are retained they are said to be aberrant and the child will retain immature patterns of behaviour because primitive reflexes prevent the development of more sophisticated postural reflexes.

The asymmetric tonic neck reflex (ATNR)

This reflex emerges in the second trimester of pregnancy when the mother feels the actions she describes as kicking. As the foetus turns its head to one side, the limbs on that side extend and the opposite ones flex. In the womb this reflex facilitates movement, develops muscle tone and stimulates the vestibular sense or balance mechanism. It plays an important part in the birth process. A full ATNR must be present if the baby is to be able to wind itself down the birth canal. If it has not developed properly then it does not fully promote the birth and forceps or a c-section may result. Interestingly, any birth trauma may prevent the inhibition of the reflex.

In the first six months the ATNR helps develop hand–eye coordination. As the baby's head turns his field of vision is extended to near and then far distance. Then the inhibition of the ATNR should occur allowing the release of the next reflex. In some children the ATNR stays active and it hinders further development. For example it is impossible to crawl using a fluent cross lateral pattern. Crawling is vital for the development of hand–eye coordination and for the integration of the vestibular sense with the other senses. It also helps myelinate the CNS. Retention affects walking too as any head turning stimulates straightening of the limbs on that side and balance is affected. Tasks such as kicking and catching a ball are carried out in a one-sided immature manner and any sense of hand dominance is delayed.

The MORO reflex

The earliest primitive reflex is the MORO (also called the flight or fight reflex). It emerges at about nine weeks in utero. This is an automatic or involuntary reaction from the brain stem to internal or external threat, e.g. hunger, cold, fear of noises, or abrupt changes in the environment. Beyond the child's conscious control, the reflex is nonetheless there to protect the child and ensure his survival. In the newborn baby the arms move symmetrically and suddenly outwards, the hands stretch, there is a pause and then the arms close in again over the body. As the arms reach out, the chest is widened to allow breathing in and exhalation in turn occurs as the arms come back over the trunk. This can explain why a failing to breathe baby gets a smack to set the MORO into action! This reflex action can be lifesaving, e.g. if the abrupt action removes a blanket that has fallen over a child's face!

At two-to-four months of age however, the baby should have developed some muscular control and become more purposeful in his actions. By then, the reflex should only come into play at times of extreme stress. It should be replaced by the adult startle reflex. But if this doesn't happen, if it remains, then the child will be hypersensitive in one or several sensory channels. Sounds, lights, changes of direction, reflections of lights on walls, buzzing radiators are all things that cause inordinate distress.

The child with a retained MORO is the over-anxious child who needs constant reassurance and attention; the child who is reluctant to stay; the child who hates any change in routine. Sound and light therapy may be required if environmental changes are not enough to reduce the sensory responses. The children are constantly on the alert. Fearing trauma, they are geared up to flee. Building relationships is also difficult as the child will be unable to countenance any suggestion of change or risk. Alternatively, the children may react by being aggressive, hitting out at those around. They wish to dominate every game. They must win. This is *why* the reflex is often called the 'fight or flight reflex'.

The early flailing of limbs should gradually develop into reaching and grasping, i.e. controlled actions. This is possible because higher levels of the brain have come into use. This means that connections to the thinking part of the brain, the cortex are developing. So the primitive reflexes that have developed in utero, that have ensured survival and assisted at the birth process should be replaced by postural reflexes that begin by promoting fundamental skills such as sitting and standing and gradually support the acquisition of more complex skills such as running and jumping or writing and dancing, i.e. those requiring coordination. These stay with the children all their lives.

Difficulties due to a retained MORO reflex: the children will be likely to:

- Be tense, ill at ease
- Have balance and coordination difficulties
- Be reluctant to join in new activities
- Withdraw from learning new things
- React aggressively; not understand conflict
- Dislike changes in routine
- Have allergies and low immunity
- Will tire easily.

As can be seen the effects of a retained MORO are profound.

The palmar reflex

The palmar reflex concerns grasping. It is thought to be a continuation of a skill needed when babies had to cling to their mother for safety. In the new baby, the palmar reflex can be seen when babies knead their hands as they suck. This should be inhibited by four to six months so that the pincer grip can begin to develop. If this doesn't happen, i.e. if the palmar reflex is retained it can have a negative effect on fine motor coordination (the child who clutches a toy or a paintbrush and has difficulty letting go), on speech and articulation (when the children attempt to draw, their tongues come out and lips are licked!) All of these can be seen in young children with learning disabilities.

Difficulties due to a retained palmar reflex:

- Poor dexterity because the fingers and thumbs are not coordinated
- The pincer grip is not developed leading to clumsiness in handling objects
- The palm may be over-sensitive (children who won't tolerate clay can use Theraputty)
- The link between grasping and kneading delays muscle control at the front of the mouth and so the development of speech is affected.

Strategies
- Pop bubble wrap to help develop the pincer grip
- Use tweezers to lift Rice Krispies
- For hand awareness, pull marshmallows apart
- Play old-fashioned rhymes such as

'Here is the church,
here is the steeple,
Open the door to
Look at the people.'

or

Ditties such as 'Five little buns in a baker's shop', or 'Here comes Peter, here comes Paul' all develop finger awareness and, if practised regularly, develop strength and dexterity.

The tonic labyrinthine reflex (TLR)

This is a reflex that emerges early in utero, and is sustained from birth and for the first three months of life. It is vitally important for the child's developing relationship with gravity. The vestibular sense or sense of balance is the only one to work before birth and it helps the foetus adopt a head down position ready to be born. This position ensures the best supply of oxygen to the baby's brain. The foetal vestibular system provides the baby with information about direction and supports head control. Until this is established, the young child cannot develop hand–eye control, visual acuity or balance securely.

Inhibition of the TLR is a gradual process. It should disappear by three years of age. If it is retained, head movement beyond the level of the spine will cause reflexive flexion and extension in the muscles at the back of the legs resulting in clumsiness and falling. The child may be stooped and floppy or be rigid and jerky. Walking, running and jumping will be done on stiff legs. The children are awkward and uncoordinated because their balance is faulty. This is critically important because being well balanced is a prerequisite of any successful movement pattern. Children with a poor sense of balance must concentrate on trying to achieve that to the detriment of other learning.

Strategies

Children with autism often have stiff legs and pitch forward when they jump from a bench. Legs have to be 'bendy' if they are to be resilient and absorb the body weight on landing. This is vital for safety. Children need support to land, even from a low height till they have a resilient landing. Thick mats should always be available.

Have 'knee awareness practices', e.g. rub your knees, make them bend and stretch – repeat. This is fun if a rhythmical jingle accompanies the practice.

Lie on back, legs bent up in front. Teacher pushes feet gently till knees are bent – child pushes them straight, then bends them again.

Stand in front of the child, take two hands and hold back the weight as the child jumps from a table in the gym.

There are many subtle reasons for children's difficulties. This is only a brief introduction. For detailed information of these and other reflexes, read any book by Sally Goddard (-Blythe) who is a key person in this field.

Chapter 4

Come and meet our older children at play

More case studies with strategies to foster development

It's time to meet Sophia, Jill, Cara, Freddy, Martin, Robbie and Freya

The first two case studies demonstrate the importance of music and rhythm for children with learning differences and autism. Grandin (2014) is investigating the therapeutic effects of singing. Hearing 'so many parents and teachers being sure that singing was really beneficial', she wondered if there could be scientific evidence to back this claim. She explained that, 'the areas of the brain that are responsible for language and music overlap to some degree, yet even non-verbal children respond well to music'. Wan (2011) created a specialised treatment where she trained children aged five to nine to 'experience the relationships between speaking at different pitches and tapping tuned electronic drum pads'. The children made significant progress in their ability to articulate words and phrases. In this study, teacher Anna inspires her children with chime bars, drumming and singing.

Case study for Sophia

Sophia is nearly ten. She finds communication so difficult that for most of the day she is withdrawn and reluctant to take part in any kind of classroom activity. She has very limited language but uses it appropriately when she can be persuaded to speak. Her teacher Anna explains that she has a very poor memory, often failing to remember – looking blank and totally unresponsive when yesterday's story or outing to the shops is recalled. Anna has used 'advance organisers' and left these with Sophia before each interaction but still she becomes distressed, biting her hands if anyone persists. This has severely affected her confidence.

And because she doesn't remember, she trails behind the other children when they go to snack or the gym and shows very little animation. She is beginning to copy, e.g. in following the others to fetch her coat before going outside, but everything appears tedious and hard work, nothing appears to give her pleasure.

She does eat crackers and crispy toast but won't have any fruit or vegetables. She finds life very hard. She responds best to music and enjoys drumming to accompany songs that play on her earphones. Her music teacher Lesley is delighted by her progress on the xylophone (just two notes but confidently and accurately played in time to a song) but at this moment in time she doesn't appear to find pleasure in anything else. However, music has established a bond between the two and the plan is to have more music each day so that Sophia can shine. Anna explains, 'We have soft music playing in class now and sometimes we see her pause to listen and we hope it gives her pleasure'.

Strategy

Remembering Leon's breakthrough when he switched off the tape recorder, and noting Sophia's awareness of the music playing, the team encouraged Sophia to switch the music off and on. This took time but she did it and found the volume buttons too. The team was delighted. She explained:

> It's the first time she has shown any purpose or motivation. She carries the tape recorder anywhere she can and it's quite hard to persuade her to leave it in the cupboard at bus time. For a time she turned the volume up and down all the time – we weren't sure whether it was the control she liked as much as the music but this has settled and now she asks for the tape, saying, 'music on' clearly. Also she remembers the cupboard where the tape is kept and how to work it. We hope that she might let another child sit by her to listen but voluntarily sharing the machine is some time away.

As part of her ASC, she demonstrates two 'differences' that worry members of the team. The first is that she still has spells of toe walking. This happens intermittently and doesn't appear to link to any particular environment or activity. Her heels can come down and physiotherapists report no shortening of her achilles tendon or muscle weakness, so she doesn't need splints. She doesn't seem to be aware of the change from the normal pattern to toe walking and it is difficult to link the change with any other happening.

Theoretic explanation for toe walking

Although at first glance, toe walking would seem to be an action that signified a good sense of balance, if it persists beyond toddlerhood, it is a physical trait that may be linked to autism and cerebral palsy. The child may have a short achilles tendon and need splints. This can also be caused by a muscular weakness that requires physiotherapy but it may be just a sign of immaturity. Sometimes toe walking disappears for no apparent reason, but early interventions making the child aware of the effective walking pattern and seeking to change the habit through fun experiences that boost her confidence is best!

Strategies to diminish toe walking

1) Sophia and the team painted some sugar paper and in bare feet Sophia walked over it making patterns. She was aware that when she toe-walked the pattern was different. She pointed to her heels and volunteered, 'lost'.
2) After washing off the paint, the team had some moisturiser 'to keep her feet soft' but really to make her aware of the different parts of her foot. Her mum was happy to do this again each night and Sophia was soothed by the attention and tolerated the tactile stimulation well.

3)   Sophia then practised pressing her bare foot onto wet sand in a tray to see if she could make the whole foot pattern. That achieved, her nursery nurse demonstrated the transition of movement from heel to toe that is part of the usual walking pattern and this was tried with exaggerated movements, e.g. pretending to walk over a sticky floor; beating the floor hard when marching and halting; taking giant steps after working with the poem, 'The Kindly Giant' in *Jingle Time* (see bibliography). The first verse is shown below.

> "There are giant footsteps on the path outside –
> a right one, a left one make one huge stride.
> What kind of size do you think the giant might be?
> Will he be taller than the highest tree?"

Sophia responded well to the one-to-one intense interaction. She particularly enjoyed marching round the gym playing her drum.

Theoretic explanation for 'one-sidedness'

The second more unusual difficulty is that Sophia tends not to use/finds it difficult to use the left side of her body. She draws with her right hand but if something she needs is on her left side, she will reach over with her right arm to grasp it. Her left arm and hand do seem floppy, possibly due to lack of use.

Anna explained:

> When it was time for her to mix the porridge (for the three bears story on porridge day), we tried to get her to hold the mixing bowl with her left arm while the right one stirred the mixture but she insisted on placing the bowl on the table, even although it moved and spilt the milk everywhere. We tried to take her right hand so that she would have to use her left to take her coat from the peg but she pulled away and ran off.
>
> The physiotherapist has checked Sophia's shoulder and thought her difficulty was down to a mild form of hemiplegia. She advised 'Sophia has to keep that shoulder moving or the muscles will atrophy'. She advised immediate and sustained intervention.

Strategies to help Sophia use both arms

1)   The PE specialist worked with the physiotherapist to devise actions that involved two arms circling and stretching forwards and backwards and then they did some Pilates stretching to music.
2)   Different members of the team played a game that punched a balloon in a balloon bag to keep it in the air. At first, till the game was established and enjoyed, Sophia just used her right arm, then the team encouraged her to use her left one. A blue band was tied around one wrist and a red one around the other and then 'RED' or 'BLUE' was called out to make the exercise into a fun game.
3)   The next idea was to have her roll a large ball around the gym. This was a mobilising rather than a strengthening activity but in error the ball rolled to the mouth

of the clear tunnel set out to encourage crawling. Mark, busy crawling through, couldn't get out! (He was amused by this, not traumatised!) Sophia pushed the ball to hold it in place while Mark pushed from the other end to escape. This was definitely strengthening work that she found fun.

4) Then Sophia faced the wallbars, climbing her fingers up as high as she could. The spot she reached with either arm was marked by a coloured band. Every day she tried to stretch to the next rung. As she was tall for her age she was pleased to see that her bands were both higher than some of the other children who joined in the game.

Checking hand and foot dominance

When physical difficulties are suspected it is important to check that the child is able to use both sides of the body. Each child will have a dominant or preferred hand, foot and eye and these may not be on the same side of the body. At around five or six years of age there is an important surge in the production of myelin when connections between the vestibular system, the cerebellum and the corpus callosum are stabilised. This is the time when dominance should be established. Children who are right-handed should use their right foot to kick a ball, primarily their right eye to spot images and the right ear for processing speech – and similarly for the left handers. This shows organisation in regions of the higher brain.

Many children will be cross lateral and cope quite well, but a clear one-sided dominance (either right or left) is beneficial. When the 'wiring' for specific tasks is encoded, movement tasks become effective and efficient. With dominance, there is no confusion/delay in selecting one side or the other.

Strategies to help children recognise which hand and foot they prefer to use

Simple games, e.g. rolling a ball to one side or the other and watching how the child deals with the catch, throw or kick, can provide useful observations. If the child uses the more appropriate side, that's good, the child will go on to develop what is known as hand or foot dominance which is a normal, positive developmental achievement for neurotypical children by age six. Especially when there are learning difficulties, however, it is essential that the two sides are checked just to ensure that both are strong enough to be used. Muscles can atrophy if they are unused, making life even more difficult.

Make sure the games are fun – this is a time for adults to observe

a) Use children's darts.
b) Have a large piece of ribbed cardboard and roll a ping pong ball down. See which hand the child naturally uses to catch it. If the catch happens before the ball reaches the ground, a point is awarded. Then the staff can ask 'which hand got the best score?' and so foster hand dominance.

Figure 4.1 Amy has crawled over from the corner to throw beanbags into the pail. She is trying out both hands to see which is easier and which gains the highest score. Thereafter her teacher will remind her to hold her pencil or brush in that hand till dominance is established and she automatically chooses her dominant side. Sometimes people who use either hand or foot will claim they are 'ambidextrous'. While in a small number of cases this will be so, it is more likely that they have mixed dominance!

Case study for Jill

Now meet Jill as she takes part in a musical interlude in the fourth class.

Teacher Lesley is very enthusiastic about her music teaching and feels that Jill, who listens carefully and seems anxious to participate, gains a great deal through learning to play the chime bars accompanying a simple song. Lesley explains, 'I know the children get pleasure from being involved in the music circle where they sing simple songs and then accompany the rhythm on chime bars. This gives them confidence that carries over into daily activities'.

She was anxious to elaborate on the multifaceted learning that was implicit in singing and playing an instrument.

She explained,

> First of all singing and learning to accompany the song is such fun. Success brings musical shivers and a boost to the self-esteem. I always ask the children, 'wasn't that great?' and when we get it right we stand and do 'musical shivers' just for fun. That encourages smiling. But there is even more than that. To take part the children have to listen and internalise the rhythm; they have to wait, watch each

other play and most of all they have to beat the correct rhythm on the chime bar. This is very good training for turn taking, so important in social and language development. Their brains are energised by a new fun experience, hopefully promoting new neuronal development and they have the pleasure of hearing the sounds and recognising when they are crisp or blurred. So we have 'good listening, good playing and good singing'.

Looking at the detail, the children must develop the pincer grip to control the thin beaters and they must control the pace and timing of each strike. They benefit from taking part in a group activity and of course learning a new skill where their bodies respond to the energy and fun.

Asked how she developed this idea, Lesley explained her strategy.

> In a small singing circle, the children sing along to the 'Hello song' (originally called 'Skip, skip, skip to my Lou'). First they learn the song – I sing it to them individually. They each have a turn with their name featuring in the song, e.g.

> Hello Jill, How are you?
> Hello Jill, How are you?
> Hello Jill, how are you?
> How are you today?

and once the first verse is learned an answer rhyme can be added,

> Jill is very well,
> Jill is very well,
> Jill is very well,
> She's very well today!

Lesley continued,

> Then the children learn to accompany the song by beating two chime bars. The two notes used are concert C and G as this perfect fifth interval arrangement allows for a see-saw effect with regards to the pitch of the song. Developments on this theme can have the children selecting a picture of a friend from the visual timetable then everyone sings the song to that friend. So the song has many different benefits.

Other rhymes can be tried, e.g.

> Listen carefully and CLAP, CLAP, CLAP,
> Listen carefully and TAP, TAP, TAP,
> Listen carefully and stamp your feet,
> Stamp your feet today.

Then there are the old favourites!

> If you're happy and you know it clap your hands
> If you're happy and you know it clap your hands
> If you're happy and you know it, then your face will surely show it,
> If you're happy and you know it clap your hands.

Songs like this help children understand that feelings and expressions go together – particularly useful for children on the spectrum. This helps self-awareness and partner awareness and reading emotions.

> If you're sad today then cry and wipe your eyes
> If you're sad today then cry and wipe your eyes
> If you're sad and you know it, then your face will surely show it
> If you're sad today then cry and wipe your eyes.

> When you're smiling again look up and grin,
> When you're smiling again look up and grin,
> If you're ready, really ready then stand up and be steady,
> Stamp your feet like this – oh what a din!!

Discussions about things that make the children happy and sad could follow if the children have speech or they can select a symbol from their PECS book.

Other favourites: Fischy Songs: e.g. 'You are a star, just the way you are' available on iTunes: https://itunes.apple.com/gb/artist/fischy-music/id332470756

Case study for eight-year-old Cara

Cara's teacher Ian reflects on her time in school. He explains,

> If you met Cara in the street, you might not guess there was something causing her difficulties. She would be very pleasant and chatty and she would invite you to her party. At a quick meeting you do not realise that she has an obsession with having a party – she knows all about organising it and keeps inviting more people. The problem is that because she can't write the details down, she has to keep them all in her mind and she worries about forgetting them. The actual party is three months away but Cara has no conception of time to ease her worries. Tomorrow and next week – they are all the same.
>
> When we had the postbox in school at Christmas, she was enchanted. At last there was somewhere handy to post her party invitations. Her brain seems 'blocked' by this whole plan – it cuts her off from new learning.

Ian was concerned that the worry of it all was overwhelming her rather than giving her pleasure. He continued, 'She is a pleasant girl who seeks out interactions with particular peers. She is anxious to be a good friend but she needs a lot of support in knowing how to interact with them'.

Ian explains that her inner thoughts and plans drive her behaviour.

> These inner drives can become obsessive at times and can predominate her mind for substantial portions of the day. She must keep talking to reassure herself and

possibly to prevent others putting forward different and to her, unacceptable ideas? This must happen at home too, but equally they can fade into the background and then she can follow an externally led agenda instead of being dominated by an internal one. At these times she can participate well in learning and play.

Generally, she finds it difficult to follow typical school routines such as hanging her coat on her peg, lining up and settling down at circle time. She can carry out each step of the routine individually but is defeated by the sequence of it all. (See Appendix 2 for photo ideas for sequences.) She has a number of set routines that monopolise her thoughts and actions although many are imaginative ideas or wishful thoughts. These are:

- Plans and details about her birthday party and who is coming to it
- A need for a plaster/cream/to see a doctor or have some other medical intervention
- A need for new items, e.g. dress, shoes, a haircut
- Having a wobbly tooth and a visit from the tooth fairy
- Getting stickers and certificates for being good
- Being a good friend – who her best friends are and their whereabouts.

Many of these thoughts evoke very emotional scenarios, e.g. she will be very excited, jumping up and down about party arrangements; she will kick or bite or insult others or cry when she doesn't win a certificate (even if she hasn't participated she insists she should have a reward!) and she constantly shows high levels of anxiety about her health.

She can chat about all of these things, but she holds a very one-sided conversation. Many of her ideas seem plausible but there is a great deal of repetition. She will use many questions, e.g. 'Will Mummy give me a plaster when I get home? Do I need new shoes?' and she continues even when no answers are forthcoming. She will look at the person she is speaking to but not wait for responses. She uses a wide ranging vocabulary but when she is anxious she repeats phrases and becomes louder and more animated over time. This can culminate in her becoming withdrawn and shut down. She does not cope with questions directly addressed to her, even 'What would you like for snack?'

Strategies to support Cara

- Use clear simple language about things happening now. She cannot appreciate ideas such as 'next week' or 'in the summer'.
- Prepare verbal options, e.g. 'Would you like crackers or fruit?' instead of leaving choices open, e.g. 'What would you like to have?'
- When Cara becomes anxious or if frustration builds up, take her on a walk round the school or show her photos till she becomes calm.
- Build picture sequences to show the steps in baking (e.g., hands washed, aprons on, fetch a spoon) and for daily routines. (The example in Appendix 2 is of a younger child but the same kind of sequence could be taken of Cara.)
- To encourage focusing, and to allay worries, have a very structured routine in a familiar environment. Analyse sequences to recognise how much remembering is involved and whenever possible, simplify the demand.

- Give praise readily whenever it is deserved – and give a sticker or some other concrete evidence that she has done well.
- Be gentle with her stories; she needs to believe in order to make sense of her world.

Ian linked this idea with 'healthy eating' and the children made a collage of plates of food 'for Cara's party'. 'When anxieties built up she could see the pictures in her scrapbook. This saved her having to remember every detail.

- For new skills learning, give 1:1 support and break down skills after a demonstration of the 'whole.'
- Be ready with favourite ploys, e.g. drawing, or take her away from anxiety-producing scenarios when things become too much.
- As Cara cannot write she needs a visual diary to ease her having to remember details.
- Help her understand about turn taking in conversations perhaps by passing a ball over when talk changes from one to the other. This can develop awareness of how long she has been speaking.
- Build a calendar of boxes and help her illustrate them, e.g. snow in January, daffodils in March, so that she can appreciate the time that has to pass before her party.

Six months on

Cara still finds change challenging and needs the security that comes from routine and familiarity. When she is in a situation where she is relaxed and happy her sense of humour comes to the fore. This has been evident with activities such as playboxes where she is working 1:1 with an adult on emerging play skills and when playing with friends. She also really enjoys drawing and looking at photos of friends and families and these are activities she will choose to do when she has free time.

Baron-Cohen (1989) advises that Cara's speech difficulties should be called 'repetitive actions'. He explains that these come about because the child does not understand her own mental states and so has to repeat her worries, preferences, pleasures to make them real.

Strategy to support the appreciation of time

The key to this, explained one parent, while others nodded, is to have a large timetable for everything.

> For Sylvie we have a large one that just shows months of the year – this helps her understand how long it is till Christmas. Then we have daily timetables where sticky notes tell her about her activities such as swimming so that she can find her bathing suit. This has really helped. She can do without her 'getting dressed' timetable now but it took a long time for her to manage. Even in the bathroom we have a chart that says 'clean your teeth alongside a picture of paste and a brush!' That strategy has saved many upsets. When she forgets how to get ready

for something, instead of doing things for her, now I say, 'Look at your chart', and she does!

(Examples are in Appendix 2.)

Case study for Freddy

Freddy is a very quiet but physically active seven-year-old boy with autism and associated communication difficulties. At the start of the year he presented as a child who could be very hard to engage and motivate; a child who preferred to quietly follow his own agenda, keeping himself occupied but otherwise disengaged in a busy classroom. Staff from his earlier class reported that while he did not offer much intentional communication, when he really wanted something he would lead an adult to it or present them with an object signifier, e.g. he would lead adults to a cupboard he wanted opened or give them a cup if he wanted a drink and happily this continues. In class today he is still not motivated to communicate verbally. His parents tell that at home he will offer a few words, e.g. 'Mummy', 'Daddy', 'car', but he has not yet spoken in school. This makes it difficult for him to explain when he is uncomfortable or unwell or for him to communicate his food/activity choices.

He can undress independently but needs support with dressing. He can cope at the toilet on his own although visits are rare. He eats well at snack and lunch but needs a lot of adult support to use cutlery; however, his attempts at eating cereal with a spoon are improving. He can learn new classroom routines through contextual cues, e.g. he will go to wash his hands when he sees snack being prepared.

Freddy is very agile and has well controlled gross and fine movement skills. He enjoys rough and tumble games and tickles and when this finishes he will move the adult's hands to request more, making good eye contact as he does so. He is very confident on the gym equipment. As this is an enjoyable strength, perhaps he could try words like 'jump' or 'roll?' He does not have the rigidity in his back that some of the other children show and can land resiliently and safely from a jump from a low table, so there would be time to focus on accompanying words. He enjoys and is competent in manipulating small objects such as clothes pegs. This favourite activity means he has good practice in using the pincer grip so this should help painting control and his drawing skills.

Strategies to develop Freddy's communication skills

Earlier attempts to use PECS in a previous class had not met with success so this was temporarily set aside until Freddy was ready. His teacher, May, used 'object signifiers', e.g. a ball for gym, a piece of fake grass for playground, a plate for snack and this gave him confidence in recognising what came first and next.

Six months on, Freddy has developed good visual discrimination skills. He can colour match and sort both independently and quickly. He can match timetable symbols and black and white numbers 1–10. Freddy's teacher is aiming to try PECS again hoping this might encourage both verbal and non-verbal communication.

May began by using laminated pictures of things Freddy had done well, and talked about these, using them as an aide-memoire to remind him of things he had achieved.

So pictures of Freddy holding his triumphs, 'I can make a beautiful picture: ride a horse confidently; enjoy messy play; choose what to do; complete a 15 part inset puzzle; run and jump and balance' were all illustrated as achievements and used as 'advance organisers' or stimuli for reminders at the start of lessons.

The team hoped that as he had a good sense of balance, he soon would be able to ride the trike, then the bicycle. The team were also concerned that they had not managed to stimulate him to play with a greater variety of toys. Would an 'Action Man' interest him?

Six months on

When a teaching session is over, Freddy now knows to take the symbol from the board and place it in the appropriate folder. He can select one or two symbols from a PECS book now to show his preferences at snack. He is quiet but, in spite of resourcing the outdoor classroom he is still not interested in play activities. He enjoys his time in the gym, preferring the free choice time to practising specific activities or following routines.

Ideas for development

1) In the gym, Ria involved Freddy in a 1:1 challenge on the climbing frame. She knew he could climb up and down safely and land well. This time he had to look to choose between bands arranged at different heights on the bars, collect just one and bring it down then hand it to a waiting friend. The other children watched from the bench, some applauding him as he climbed. Ria demonstrated the climbing and Freddy copied this with no hesitation, but after climbing down, wouldn't pass his trophy on. So while the physical skill was practised, the communication one was lost.

2) After a lively spell on the trampoline, Ria, hoping that Freddy was ready to try something new, was anxious to try a game where he had to cooperate with another boy to make the game work. Reuben, who has Down's syndrome and who had already practised the game, was his partner. The two children had to crawl towards one another on mats and then climb up onto a flat gym table, balancing alongside one another to pass before jumping off or climbing down to finish. The idea was that they would watch each other and time the phases so that they were together on the table top. With two adults standing by the table, Freddy was persuaded to wait for Reuben on the table top, then they clambered down in opposite directions. There was enough of a movement challenge to keep Freddy motivated and after a few turns and explanations, his awareness of Reuben significantly increased. Game over he went to stand near Reuben and later sat beside him for snack.

Case study for Martin

Martin is a ten-year-old who has Down's syndrome. He is happy to come to school and is anxious to make friends, but he finds learning difficult so, like other children, he has special assistance, e.g. with speech and language therapists and physiotherapists sharing their expertise with the team as well as giving him individual weekly support. Martin is making very pleasing progress, speaking with more people especially those that give him time to form his words without flustering him and so his articulation is improving. He has special activities, e.g. blowing bubbles, chewing brown bread, and these strengthen the muscles in his mouth. He has been in hospital for several long spells but at last his major health problems have responded to treatment and he is getting stronger and sturdier. He still has regular hospital checks which require time off school, but the gap between visits is increasing.

He is quite tall and slim for a child with Down's syndrome, because many, even most of the children tend to be smaller and often quite plump, yet the team have been asked to be careful with his diet as he really enjoys his food and could become overweight, which might hamper his activity. He tries to avoid games and projects outside and finds going to the gym upsetting because he lacks early experience and finds balancing a problem. Simple team games, e.g. throwing a beanbag over a bench for another child to throw back, are also difficult possibly because the sequence defeats him. He has spectacles and would have difficulty in timing an approaching ball especially if it depended on peripheral vision. He does enjoy batting a balloon in a bag with one of the team who keep it on track and he laughs heartily if the balloon floats away or if it bursts.

Figure 4.2 Martin's maths is supported by the visual method Numicon.

He still has difficulty hearing clearly in spite of having grommets. This is why visual learning dominates his timetable. In the picture you see Martin using Numicon, a method of teaching maths that is both visual and interactive.

Apart from recognising more number patterns, his fine motor skills are developing as he has to use the pincer grip and there are precision demands in placing the pieces on the fret. He can now 'give me two grapes' accurately without the fret and can add confidently with it. So just like using the PECS symbols, the team contextualise his number learning and explain transfer, i.e. how the number two can refer to different articles in the shop as well as biscuits on his plate.

Indoors, he is keen to play. He loves tea parties in class and happily plays in the mud kitchen getting things ready. He is anxious to include other children and is just beginning to understand that a child wandering away is not a personal slight. He is beginning to be interested in books and can read some words. This has been supported by his iPad Early Reading programme that he can access independently.

Strategies

1) The team are concentrating on teaching specific life skills, e.g. making a sandwich independently. This involves washing lettuce and chopping hard boiled egg in a cup before spreading it on the bread. He enjoys baking sponge cakes where he has to mix the butter and weigh out flour. He is reading simple picture recipes and is delighted for the other children to share his baking at snack time.

2) Martin particularly enjoys art and collage making. The class have made a colourful collage of 'friendly fish' following a story and Martin informs everyone who passes, 'these are my fish'. He also enjoys popping bubble paper and rolling colour over it to represent the sea. While it is satisfying to have a colourful and

Figure 4.3 Colour rolled over bubble paper gives a realistic setting for the cut out fish.

attractive end product, a key aim of his art work is to mobilise and strengthen his hands that have a deep simian crease which hinders his dexterity.

3) He is learning to crawl and the team hope this will help his coordination and his tracking skills.

Case study for Robbie

Robbie at 12 years, is in the senior class at this school. Previously in mainstream education, he has been here for two years and has responded well to 1:1 interaction. His teacher Catriona and nursery nurse Kathryn describe him.

He is a very willing, amenable boy, especially if a game with his planes is on the cards. He brings his favourite planes into school and is anxious that they are lined up properly before he goes to lessons. He does allow another child to play with them in his presence, but they have to respect his toys. Mid air crashes are not allowed. He is intrigued by cars and all kinds of mechanical things that make a noise and his teacher is working on increasing his vocabulary that describes sounds, e.g. whirr, squeak, rumble.

His language is good – he talks readily about things in his personal life and things he wants to have, going into quite a bit of detail, sometimes using his imagination to embellish his stories. He is friendly and curious when strangers come into the room so there are no immediate barriers to break down. He is very independent, often not wanting to listen to instructions and not requesting help. He can be really determined and it has taken some time for him to understand and follow the school routine and understand the boundaries we set to keep everyone safe. He has no fear and sometimes his excitement spills over, so we have to set clear boundaries and get him to respect them. We are anxious about road safety and are working on 'STAY SAFE' strategies. This is vital as he goes to secondary school soon and will meet many new challenges.

He has a good appetite and whether he brings a packed lunch or has a school meal, he enjoys his food and will chat about what he had. Yet sometimes he is tired and off colour and we know he has spells of being very unwell so we have to be very vigilant. His tiredness affects his concentration and he can easily go off track. It's hard to get him to focus but we have books that show engines and airplanes and these will hold his attention for a time. Academically, he can now write his first name without support and is working on his second name. He can recognise numbers up to 20 and he knows colours and 3D shapes. He can add and take away within ten using practice materials and recognises coins. He can follow three key word instructions when he is focused and has finished Set 1 sounds from our literacy programme. He is working on Set 2, which includes blends.

It can be hard to keep him focused so lessons have to be short with breaks, preferably something totally different such as running outside and climbing on the apparatus there, or taking him into the gym. It's his being aware of dangers that worry us. If we explain this he will show us his muscles but we don't see any improvement in him taking care.

Strategy: asking Robbie to keep other children safe

1)   As Robbie is Primary 7 now, we were anxious to find how he would respond to being given more responsibility and hoped this could incorporate appreciating risks and keeping safe. So we made him 'in charge' of taking some of the younger carefully chosen children from their classes to the school door and later, with adult supervision onto the school bus. He had to demonstrate how to wait in line patiently, check that the door was held open safely, that the children's coats and bags were fastened and they were ready to go home. This was a very useful planning and sequencing activity. He remembered all day that he had to collect certain children – 'Is it time yet?' – and was very responsible in making them wait at the door of the school. He followed this sequence carefully but we are not yet sure whether this has influenced his own behaviour. This is another example of transfer not really being understood, but we go on trying.

2)   Robbie's new questioning about time, 'Is it time yet?', was the stimulus for this development which Kathryn devised.

In class there was a linear visual timetable with PECS symbols showing the events of the day. In order to make this a 'transfer of learning' opportunity, the team decided to try producing a clock face, firstly putting events (PECS symbols) round and then using clock hands. The children know that at 10am they had snack so when George the nursery nurse turned the hands to 10am, Robbie found the symbol for snack and attached that to the velcro on the clock face. Gradually, items were replaced and the team voted that the children were more appreciative of the passing of time. Later the symbols were not required as the children came to associate the clock hands e.g. pointing to three o'clock and getting ready to go home.

This took time and energy and patience but the team considered it had been worthwhile!

Case study for Freya

Freya is nine and she very anxious to be a good friend. Her teacher Graeme explains her difficulties and the strategies he has tried to support her.

Freya, who has autism, experiences high levels of anxiety and this impacts on all aspects of her day in school. She constantly calls out phrases or repeatedly asks questions about things she is interested in although they are not part of what we are doing. She becomes louder and more forceful throughout the day. Eventually, this causes her either to withdraw or scream and an adult has to take her for a stroll out of doors so that she has a total change of scene. Freya has significant difficulties in following a routine and needs adult support with self care skills such as hand washing, getting dressed after gym or gathering her belongings ready to go home. These are things where adult support can be quite subtle, although our other children might not notice or resent her having extra help. That's the wonderful thing about our children. They are never jealous or resentful of each other. No-one ever says 'Be quiet' or gets annoyed.

Freya is very anxious to be a good friend. She wants recognition for this but doesn't understand that giving a hug – especially if it is too strong – or staying too close to another child is not an appropriate way to demonstrate friendship. She finds it difficult to understand 'gentle'. She also finds listening really difficult; she talks over any contributions her peers make and becomes increasingly loud.

On Fridays the school hands out friendship tokens at assembly to promote positive behaviour. These are for shining examples of friendly behaviour rather than for everyday kindness. Freya talks about getting a token all week and becomes really distressed when she doesn't get one even although 'I've been good friends all week'. She leaves the assembly in tears and it is hard to comfort her by explaining that her friends didn't have a token either.

How was this to be resolved? Graeme shares his ideas.

Strategies

1) We developed a friendship system in class so that the time waiting for recognition was reduced. The team was anxious that this might give Freya more things to worry about but so far, so good.
2) We listed a number of 'favours' (the children's choice of word) and concentrated on one at a time so that there was a change of focus. These were

- saying kind words
- lips closed when friends are talking
- sharing toys
- waiting patiently for a turn
- using gentle hands
- using 'high fives' instead of hugs
- not going too close to a friend.

In class, each child has a 'jigsaw' that is completed when six 'favours' are won. This lets each child see their progress and when the jigsaw is complete, the good news transfers over to gain an award at assembly.

As the week goes on we try to give the children explicit rather than general praise to be sure they understand the favours, e.g. Freya thought her 'hard hugs' were 'gentle' so she had to be helped to understand through stroking toys and holding marshmallows. Lining up to go to snack also gave us a chance to talk about 'good spaces' and we hoped that this would help her recognise that others wanted to protect their personal space.

Graeme's recommendation?

Never think the children understand concepts that we take for granted. We need to spell out what kindness is and help them recognise how other children respond to kind behaviour – how this makes life pleasant for us all. If they don't understand, how can they change in any meaningful way? This is particularly difficult when children have autism because one child can make a real effort to be kind and the recipient ignores the gesture and wanders off. Teaching these children can be perplexing if you don't learn to see the world through their eyes. It's not easy, but so revealing and so rewarding when we get it right and the child copes better, even in small ways. And often the children surprise us, they really do!

Graeme has tackled the key social competence that besets many children, i.e. 'how to make a friend', by analysing what is involved and gradually explaining all the competences that are taken for granted in the non-autistic world. His own understanding has been enriched by 'trying to see the world through the children's eyes' and by relishing what others might see as small gains in the hope that 'the light will somehow be switched on' and the children will learn to be happy and proud.

Chapter 5

Theoretical underpinnings for the second selection of strategies

Memory: transfer of learning from one situation to another

Habituation

There have been years of debate when academics have tried to define intelligence, many analyses that attempt to separate out the different, necessary components and many critiques of the tests that have been devised and used. The Wechsler Intelligence test for children, which has some verbal subtests and which depends on the social ability to copy and internalise skills from other people, gives very different scores from the Raven's progressive matrices test that is purely non-verbal (Grandin 2014:118).

It has been fascinating to see IQ scores (based on verbal and reasoning ability as the key definition of being clever), being expanded to embrace more practical attributes, e.g. musical intelligence or social intelligence and subtle qualities such as leadership being recognised as key attributes. However, for me, one of the most fascinating definitions was made by Hein (2005) when he wrote, 'intelligence is the ability to respond appropriately in any situation'.

And surely this is a critical deficit in children with ASCs? And this must be at least partially caused by a poor memory? So pursuing that idea, the next step must be to ask, 'What abilities/skills/competences do children need to allow them to do just that, i.e. to respond appropriately?'

First, they need to be able to remember what they did on a previous occasion and then recognise the similarities between that, the new environment and the new task. Then they must transfer that learning so that it 'fits'. In so doing this will probably require either a little or even major amendment to suit the different situation and demand but the essence of the response, i.e. the underlying competences will stay the same.

The first part of this is being able to remember. How dreadful must it be not to be able to recall what was learned the day before or previously, i.e. to have a poor memory. How awful to know that people who don't understand are disguising their frustration when they imply, 'How do you not know that? You understood it yesterday! You remember how to ride your bike and you remember the way home, how is it that?'

Memory

It is because memory is many different things. It is the picture that recalls good and bad past times. It is the surge of happiness that came from being praised; it is the dread of facing a trip to hospital because of remembering the pain and what happened there; it is the feeling of peace and contentment that comes from recalling an open fire or a soothing piece of music; it is riding a bicycle or driving a car without long reflections on how it is done; it is knowing facts, e.g. that 2+2=4 or that the River Thames flows through London. It is the thing that allows accurate and realistic prediction of the future because this is based on what went on in the past. For those on the spectrum, some of whom have superb memories, it could be the thing that enabled them to recall what they read ten weeks ago – in detail – when non-autistics struggled to do so.

Amongst those who have categorised the different kinds of memory, Carter (2000) offers these definitions and descriptions. She calls the four main types of memory 'procedural, fear, episodic, and semantic'. It is important to discover which kind is deficit in learning differences so that interventions can be timely and appropriate.

- Procedural memories: these are the memories of riding a bike, driving a car, skating, i.e. the 'how to do' memories of physical skills that are stored in the cerebellum and putamen. If there is no problem the skills can be recalled with little ado. Some of these skills, e.g. walking, running, are an innate part of development. They are not taught. Other skills need a great deal of careful teaching but once acquired they stay and can be used again even after a long period of non-use.
- Fear memories, i.e. unhappy recall. These include flashbacks and phobias, and negative depressive thoughts. These are stored in the part of the brain called the amygdala. In children with autism, where the amygdala is thought to be shaped differently, the chance is that 'fear memories' become so prevalent that they override pleasant events leading to sadness or anxiety that is hard to wash away.
- Episodic memories: these are the memories formed by personal past experiences; they are clothed in personal detail. They are set in time - you were there and you were emotionally involved and so remember much more than bare facts. Carter explains that when these memories are recalled, they recreate the time and place where they were laid down. They are reinforced by the emotions that they generated. In his famous book, *A la Recherche du temps perdu*, Proust eats a small cake – a madeleine – and recalls the garden where he had a picnic, the smell of the flowers in the garden, the sunny day and the happiness of the occasion. This richness was an episodic memory. These are encoded by the hippocampus and stored in the cerebral cortex. Children with autism find such recall problematic.
- Semantic memories: these are the ones that concern the retention of facts. Rote learning comes into this category and they allow quick recall. However, children with or without learning difficulties often 'parrot' facts with pride and enjoyment without understanding what they mean. Factual recall also lays down the pegs on which elaborations can be hung. Routines that give order to the day are an example of this. Certainly children with ASCs gain confidence from knowing what the day holds. Understanding this allows them to relax rather than be fearful of change. Some children with high functioning autism, previously called Asperger's syndrome, can amass a huge number of facts. A small number – about 5 per cent are called 'mono savants' because they have prodigious memories or very high levels of skill, usually in a narrow field.

And so there are different kinds of memory beyond the well-known short and long term memories. They are stored in many different regions of the brain and they are retrieved in different ways. When a memory is laid down, an association between a group of neurons or thinking cells creates a specific pattern. One pattern brings about the memory of a note of music; another pattern from a different area in the brain raises fears and warnings; yet another will stimulate friendship or a taste of a fruit or a different food. These patterns remain in the brain after the initial stimulus has ceased. When the pattern is regularly repeated the neurons fire together strongly and it becomes encoded. The old adage 'practice makes perfect' is a truism based on this!

The human brain holds millions of these patterns or impressions. Some are transient because they have not involved much concentration, i.e. they are short term and so they can be washed away while others remain for a lifetime. They are more likely to remain if there is a personal association. So the note of music you hear may conjure up a picture of the first time you were taken to the ballet and saw the boxes in the theatre. You remember all the excitement of going and who took you there. You recall the atmosphere in the auditorium and even the taste of the drink you had at the interval! This may make you happy or sad, even resentful if the much wanted repeat visit didn't materialise.

Winston (2004) claims that cultural rituals have the same effect. The 'unusualness' helps the memory endure, perhaps forever. This is why children with complex needs should not be denied any colourful experiences because they might be overwhelmed by what is going on. Certainly this explains why children should be involved in exciting events, e.g. going carol singing. Although they may not remember the words of all the songs, there are so many different stimuli for remembering the participation, the colour and the community.

So perhaps more stress on recalling the excitement and detail of 'events' will help children with autism remember more? However, affected children may have a different perception. They seem to miss the personal or psychological details while focusing on the mechanical ones. One child with Asperger's syndrome when asked by his mother, 'Did you see the road accident as you came home?', replied, 'There were two fire engines and the ambulance had flashing lights'. The thought of people being injured had not crossed his mind at all. He was not emotionally tied in to the scene and so had lost the meaning that would have upset the neurotypical child and set the memory into the hippocampus. Why should this be?

Carter (2000) explains the theory of 'weak central coherence'. This is when observations made by children with autism do not strive for personal meaning of the 'whole' but instead see a myriad of details. As a result some children can remember and repeat strings of unconnected words or do jigsaw puzzles with ease. Sometimes these feats of memory, e.g. remembering timetables for trains, can lead to a good job, while other traits, e.g. collecting used stamps, would be less useful unless of course they happened to include rare specimens and became a philatelist's dream.

So professionals, listening to children remembering, have to ask them to elaborate, perhaps through providing prompts or questioning the things they have missed and explain why they are important. After the child's response about the traffic accident, prompts, e.g. 'How do you think the boy who was hurt was feeling? What about his Mum? Do you think the boy was in pain? How would he feel about going to hospital?', might help children with autism develop a ToM.

Habituation

The ability to habituate also depends on remembering what went before and impairment here really impedes efficiency, e.g. think of a neurotypical child climbing up and down stairs. The first time, footsteps may be tentative and unsteady and children may use a step together pattern while clutching a stair rail. The action is slow and deliberate. But after a few tries this becomes easier and the up and down journey is quicker and more efficient. Thereafter the child can adapt the learned pattern to tackle stairs and steps with different risers and treads so that there is no need to go back to the initial stumbling stage and gradually climbing and jumping in the outdoors becomes a natural extension, often done well without needing to be specifically taught. This process is called habituation.

Unfortunately, children with dyspraxia and other neurological conditions find that habituation doesn't come naturally. They don't seem to be able to remember and adapt, and each activity must be tackled as a first time try. They take longer, they stumble, they are always last in a game or in completing any task and recognising their inability without being able to 'sort it', they are often totally frustrated – or their parents, school friends and teachers are!

So, how can we help children to remember and how can we help children to transfer what they have learned in one situation to another so that they do not have to begin every new episode as a first time try, for difficulties here can be quite debilitating.

Strategies

1) Use visual timetables at home and at school – for everything!
2) Colour code everything that moves from home to school – socks, books, lunch box, gym kit etc. Use the child's favourite colour to motivate the child to use the markers!
3) Once the child has learned to match coloured items this learning can be developed in ways that help ease remembering routine, e.g. a coloured thread tied round the hanging loop of a jacket can be matched to one tied on the peg. A red dot on a snack or lunch box can provide easy identification and it can be readily placed in a bag that also has a marker. With simple identifications like these, tasks that confuse can be simplified and give the child a measure of independence.

Developing a Theory of Mind

Children with ASCs do not intuitively understand that other people may have a different view of the world from their own; that others have different feelings, concerns and preferences, different views as to what is important and trivial and different gestures to express their wishes and beliefs. And because they don't appreciate this, they find it impossible to empathise with their points of view. The instinctive ability to know what another person is thinking is known as 'ToM'. Even children on the spectrum who are 'high functioning' (i.e. they have a higher and sometimes much higher IQ score and fluent if pedantic language) also find it difficult to read facial expressions and non-verbal communications and so have similar social difficulties. (See Appendix 1.) And as 90 per cent of the meaning in a communication comes through the non-verbals, it is not difficult to appreciate the perplexities that come with ASCs, e.g. the bewilderment when a proffered interaction is met by non-comprehension or hostility because it is inappropriate for the moment at hand. Constant rejection can prevent children interacting at all. Jane Asher (2002), President of the Autistic Society, explains that because of the inability to read and respond to signals, some children 'will be locked into a silent terrifying world where nothing and no-one makes sense'. How frightening that is.

Children with autism do feel emotions themselves and many have strong attachments to other people. Their difficulties come in communicating their feelings and understanding those of others, even recognising that these others have the capacity to feel emotions. And as they also cannot interpret the emotional expressions on the faces of others and react appropriately, this can make them appear unresponsive and uncaring. Their responses – or lack of them – can mystify or even anger those who do not understand. Sadly, other children can be confused too and not knowing how to cope, they go off and leave the affected children alone.

Even more perplexing for those striving to explain and those so anxious to understand is the fact that different emotions – happiness, sadness, anger and fear – can be conveyed by different expressions, and gestures can agree or conflict with the facial cues. This is called meta incongruence. This will also affect their responses both in creating stories and understanding those heard in class.

Harris and Lipian (1989) explain, 'If children cannot understand the motives and desires of others, their stories are going to be devoid of psychological colour' – hence the child who talked about the accident with no reference to how the people involved would be feeling. They claim that children with autism are able to understand the physical and mechanical aspects of the world but lack understanding of the psychological one.

Paediatricians reflecting on the early behaviour of babies who go on to have autism, share the observation that they only looked at the lower half of their mother's faces, missing the messages that come through eye contact. Yet Charlotte Moore (2012) explains that her profoundly autistic son George sought out eye contact and fixed her attention for a considerable time, much longer that one would expect from a new baby. So there are differences. Baron-Cohen (1997) speaks of 'the language of the eyes' and claims that 'people with autism and Asperger's syndrome do not know this language'.

At a superficial level some children can recognise facial expressions that express obvious emotions, e.g. they can attach the word angry to the picture of a static face, but when the emotions are complex or changing, they can be lost.

How does this affect the children's ability to be involved in pretend/symbolic play?

Leslie (1987) hypothesises that children with autism cannot 'disengage from reality', a process required for pretending. Whereas neurotypical children will use one object as another – and temporarily believe that this is true, children with autism find great difficulty in adopting this false belief. So while they may follow instructions to 'put the car into the garage' (one made by a rectangle of coloured bricks) readily, they will not be able to empathise with the pride – or relief of the driver of the car who drove it! This is an example of functional play. Pretend play, however, has two classifications, i.e. functional and symbolic play. Symbolic play is the more sophisticated type as it requires the child to treat an object as if it were something else – the most usual example given is treating a banana as a telephone. The child must 'decouple', i.e. forgo the idea that the banana is fruit so that it can become a telephone. Inability to do this is impairment in metarepresentation which means that the children cannot imagine the perspective of others and this contributes to their difficulties in producing imaginary play. Several studies are trying to evaluate the relationship between ToM and pretend play in autism (Rutherford *et al.* 2007).

Using iPads to encourage speech

When I asked Paul, a young boy with learning difficulties (not ASCs), why he liked his laptop so much, he replied, 'Computers don't have moods!' A telling response if ever there was one! Pressed to elaborate, he explained that, if he used his laptop,

- he could anticipate what would happen
- he could control the pace of new input and
- he did not have to cope with interventions
- he felt confident when spell check was available
- he could make his presentations attractive.

Considering these for children with ASCs, there seem to be significant benefits especially with timing and pacing of learning. However, computer based methods of teaching and learning have been criticised for encouraging isolation, for apart from sitting alone, there is no shared learning with other members of the class or conclusions that might promote interactions and discussions. But surely balance in timetabling is the key here? Other teachers working with iPads also found that organisation was problematic. Tanya, responsible for Primary 4 in this school explained, 'The visuals move too fast and the children become bewildered. They tussle to get the iPad then abandon it with little gain.' Another teacher, Ian, who had a large touch screen in his classroom also was doubtful, 'On the face of it this is a marvellous resource, but I get it set up or the children do and then when things are moving, one of them touches the screen and everything disappears. Then there's mayhem!'

However, the team wanted to give individual iPads a try. This was because they had been intrigued by children who appeared to be able to speak when they were highly motivated to get their own way! Callum repeated 'bubbles on' in the sensory room, although this was his only verbal input at that time. Mia's comment was 'shoes off' as her group approached the soft play area and the team were astounded because her reply to the question, 'What would you like?' meaning biscuit or cheese and anticipating that she would choose one without speaking, was 'make-up!' So the team felt the children had potential for more speech if they could discover how to elicit it.

Lara, the teacher in the room with the first class, was convinced that two of her silent or whispering boys were 'really learning' and she was so worried that as yet she had not found a way to give them the motivation to talk. Jacob was already anxious to work the computer – he was the child who shrugged off help, made up his own passwords and became frustrated when they didn't work! So an iPad would be motivating for him.

The team also hoped that the link with switches (remember Leon's breakthrough in communication when he switched off the tape recorder?) might happen again because the touch on the screen made something happen. The investigation was planned to use videos of the children themselves as a starter.

Strategy

The outdoor play scenarios that were filmed to show the children's participation and pleasure were used as the motivating source for the investigation. The children were familiar with the environment and the resources so there were no contaminating variables. The team reviewed the videos that could be paused and prepared simple questions, hoping that the children would come to respond verbally. The team ascertained first that the children could recognise themselves and the other children on a moving screen, e.g. 'Who is this big boy on the bike?' Do you think he is happy? Look, Jamie wants to play on the bike too. Is that alright?' The children were used to having pictures and videos taken but these had been mainly used for visual displays. The team wondered how they would respond to verbal prompts.

There was no doubt that some of the children recognised themselves and the others in the class. They smiled and some could call out names but others appeared mesmerised by the movement on the screen and gave no indication of recognising anyone. They had had many opportunities to see 2D pictures but this was the first time the iPad was used in this way. Interestingly, at the start, Leon would not have anything to do with the iPad, pushing it away when a child tried to show that he had recognised him on the screen. However, when he saw the others were intrigued he gradually approached the group and now, although he doesn't speak, he is happy to have his turn looking at the screen then passing the iPad over.

The team were delighted with the animation the iPad engendered. Kieran and Mia, the two youngsters who had some language, appeared highly motivated. 'Here's Kieran on the bus' exclaimed Kieran, and he nodded his head to show he thought Kieran looked happy. Mia didn't immediately speak but stayed focused on the episode for some time. That in itself was an achievement. Later in the day she used her PECS book to request the iPad again. One or two of the children were not interested at all. Liam kept pointing to Archie as if to ask, 'Why do I need to look at a screen when he's here?!' Why indeed!

The parents were pleased that technology was being used more in the classroom, perhaps feeling that another learning tool would offer the possibility of faster achievement or perhaps they would feel that a new skill was being mastered or that they would have something to talk about with their friends, the implication being that using technology meant progress. There are of course children with ASCs and other complex needs who do very well with technology, even as a career and both the parents and the team wanted their children to have every opportunity to try.

Building movement competence and competence in children with autism

Children with ASCs will walk and run and use cutlery and other tools, but at the lower end of competence. An out of date but apt parlance would say that many were 'clumsy'. While efficient and effective movement is critically important in its own right, movement competence is pervasive and any negative effects spill into all the other aspects of learning. More positively, gains made in the movement aspect can have important benefits right across the spectrum too! For 'being in control' of their bodies gives children confidence; they feel capable and this enhances their self-esteem, fostering both emotional and hopefully social development. Once they have achieved the basic movement patterns, e.g. crawling, walking, and running, throwing and catching a ball as discrete skills, they can tackle more complex undertakings; they can run and jump and kick a ball and join in a game; they can play safely on large apparatus outside. 'Being a competent mover' is so important in all children but even more so when children have complex needs, for movement competence is public and so contributes to the feel-good factor, resulting in a positive self-esteem.

Controlled movement results when the child is well balanced and uses the correct amount of strength and speed to achieve an efficient, rhythmical action. Poor control (loss of balance and using either too much or too little strength and speed) results in bumping into others, getting bruised and generally feeling hurt and inadequate and this can cause children to withdraw from activities that might result in being hurt again.

It is important to remember that very many children on the spectrum have difficulties in planning and sequencing movements, i.e. knowing what comes first and then next and how long each will take. Not being able to copy more efficient children doesn't help. This is different from being able to carry out a demonstrated discrete skill. Teaching should consider planning and sequencing difficulties and it would be useful for teachers to talk about 'now' and 'next', 'yesterday' and 'long ago'.

Strategy

Activities like this one, where Simon is estimating the number of small steps and then strides he will need to cross the road (see p. 93), can ask children to think of 'how' movement is done, i.e. motor planning.

Mental preparation is essential in planning and if children can speak, having them verbalise their intention can be so revealing, pinpointing the kind of support/advice that is required.

What are the key movement competences? These are:

- balance
- strength and speed
- body awareness
- spatial awareness
- rhythm and coordination
- control
- movement planning and sequencing.

The first and most fundamental is balance, because this is essential for stability. Until balance is established and becomes automatic, concentration is pulled away from focusing on the task at hand. Concentration has to spend energy keeping the body upright, safe and secure.

There are two different kinds of balance and one or other is part of everything we do. Static balance lets us control our bodies when they are still or at rest. Being still is

Figure 5.1 As Simon plans his small step and large step crossings (the ropes can be moved apart as confidence grows), think also of the dynamic balance challenges he meets. The activity also develops body awareness so although the exercise looks simple, there are subtle important gains to be made. Anyone who doubts this should try it themselves! The team, looking for opportunities to explain 'transfer of learning', can relate this episode to real life 'crossing the road' situations.

amazingly hard for some children who readily topple over or look for handholds to keep erect. This can be seen when children simply cannot sit or stand still, even for a moment. They have to move so that their proprioceptors are energised to feedback positional information, in other words to tell them where they are functioning in the space around them.

Then there is dynamic balance that works to keep us in control as we move. It works all day every day, even during the night if the sleeper is at all restless. Think of the athlete and ballet dancer. They have exquisite balance that appears effortless but really comes from endless hours of sustained practice. Interestingly, when children have difficulties with dynamic balance they often try to go faster . . . almost struggling to finish the task before the balance runs out. This of course leads to lack of control and falling over.

Strength and speed (together they give rhythm and coordination)

The first assessment should be to find whether the child has enough strength to fulfil the task and if not to simplify the task or change the resources. General activity can give more fun strengthening the muscles than repeating a specific activity that proved difficult. This can come later once strength is built up. Physiotherapists can then work with teachers of physical education to ensure that the best programme is sustained on a daily basis. Strength is best developed by providing some resistance so that the muscles have to work harder.

Strategies: consider the resources

Ask the children to:

a) Use a heavy brush to sweep the playground or path with uneven stones.
b) Face the wall bars. Hold on at shoulder height and move the feet back then pull in again.
c) Walk through deep water in the swimming pool to strengthen legs.
d) Sit with legs stretched out in front. Lift one leg, then the other, then both together.
e) Hold onto the back of a chair and run on the spot.
f) Pop bubble paper – children who like 'pops' and switches particularly enjoy this!
g) Open clothes pegs to hang dolls' clothes on a line.
h) To strengthen muscles in the mouth to help the development of language, blow bubbles through a straw, or blow to keep a balloon in the air.
i) Blow pingpong balls along a table into a net.
j) Chew brown bread.

Letting go

Some children, however, use too much strength and have difficulty releasing the pencil or spoon in time. Some will be put off trying by using heavy resources, and, e.g., it is not difficult in teaching throwing and catching to replace a ball with a balloon in a bag. This travels more slowly so that the children learn the movement pattern, then when they have the idea, the ball can be replace the balloon.

Strategies: to prevent using too much strength

a) Pat dampish sand into a castle – too much strength will spoil it!
b) Play stalking games, e.g. moving without making a sound.
c) Pour water slowly so that it trickles into a narrow phial or jug.
d) Draw on paper with carbon paper underneath – try not to let the mark rub through.

Cephalo-caudal and proximo-distal development of strength and control

In the baby, strength develops from head to toe (cephalo-caudal) and from centre to periphery (proximo-distal). This explains why babies can hold their head up before they sit and all babies sit before they stand, and stand steadily before they can join two locomotor movements together. The developmental pattern that can be missed is crawling, otherwise the sequence is the same for everyone. Times for achieving the changes are called 'the motor milestones' (see Appendix 3) and while the normal time to change from one skill to the next is wide, the chart gives an immediate view as to whether movement difficulties are present or looming.

The importance of being able to crawl is already documented with the implications of difficulties recorded to show the link with other aspects of development. And this interplay is part of every other movement too. Think of a child learning to catch a ball. Hopefully he will find that catching and then learning to throw sympathetically to a partner will develop communication (the child has to look and gauge direction, strength and pace to suit a partner) and when someone calls out 'good shot' he will feel pleasure in accomplishing a task. Once ball control is established then kicking a ball into a goal can follow and the children will realise (with explanations of transfer where necessary) that they are acquiring the skills of a team game.

Precursors to throwing

Children with ASCs who find it difficult to work above eye level will find that a bouncing practice (bounce and catch individually, then to a friend) helps tracking. The two step bounce also gives more time for the ball to land into the basket made by the child's hands. Or, have the child sit with legs apart and roll the ball into the 'trap'. Legs can swing in to trap the ball just for fun! This establishes eyes following the path of the ball and gives the receiver time to clutch it and get ready to return. If this is still too fast, substitute a beanbag. Although this can be quite difficult from a sitting position, it saves chasing an out-of-control ball.

And then there are the 'I can' contributions, e.g. I can follow instructions, I can take turns, I can start, stop and move in space, which align with the play curriculum. These are very important issues in learning to move in a social environment.

Activities for children with complex needs

Activities for early years children

1. Gross motor skills

Walking
Rope or coloured tape on the floor

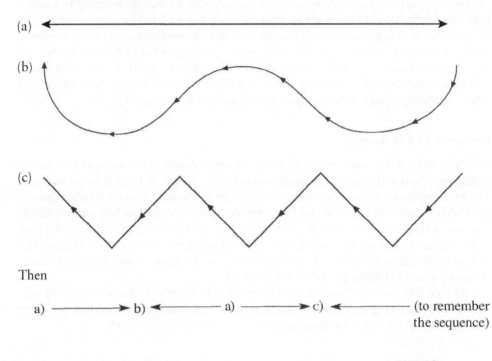

Then

a) ———————▶ b) ◀——————— a) ———————▶ c) ◀——————— (to remember
the sequence)

	HELPS
In a), encourage the children to walk carefully alongside the line, not necessarily on it, with a heel-toe action.	Body awareness
(b) and (c) are more challenging due to the gentle then acute changes of direction.	Propulsion
Encourage the children to move carefully and slowly, emphasising walking tall.	Good posture
Progression 1: two children begin at different places and watch each other, aiming to finish at the same time.	Timing

Progression 2: substitute crawling in (a). This is
very important for coordination and vital if there
is no climbing equipment.

Crawling

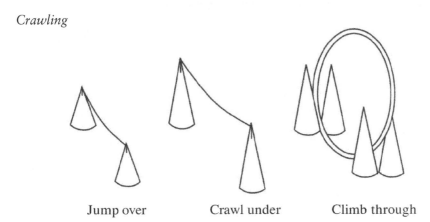

Jump over   Crawl under   Climb through

Add several hoops to crawl through.

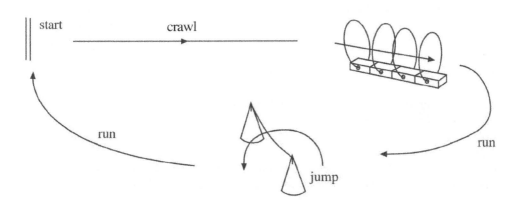

	HELPS
Children try not to touch the hoops. Emphasise 'through', 'under' and then 'over'.	Coordination, directionality
Encourage children to call out directions as they move.	Conceptual understanding of spatial terms
Progression: children rearrange apparatus and remember spatial concepts.	Development of ordering

Crawling and climbing
Crawl over a soft rolled up mat (carpet)
Crawl/climb up stairs (no hands as progression)
Jump down into a good space and run round to begin again.

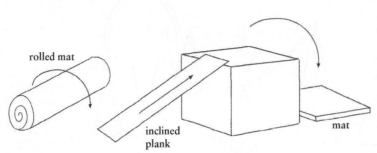

rolled mat

inclined
plank

mat

HELPS

Sequencing

Climbing actions
using the
recovery to aid
the preparation
of the next action

Progression:

Bunny jump over rolled carpet

HELPS
Strengthening
wrists (weight-
bearing)

This is a good visual sequence of activities.

Emphasise standing well – (pushing the back of the
head up) to begin and finish.

Marching and waiting
It is important that the following activities are done calmly and carefully with no
rush! 'Standing tall' gives an important sense of poise and body awareness.

HELPS

For four- and five-year-olds

Rhythmical
awareness

March forward smartly for four steps and 'wait, wait, wait'.

Control

March backwards for four steps and 'wait, wait, wait'.

Listening skills

Repeat adding a clap on the wait.

Teacher counts out rhythmically:

1 2 3 4 and wait, wait, wait
Back 2 3 4 and wait, wait, wait
Forward 2 3 4 and clap, clap, clap
Back 2 3 4 and clap, clap, clap.

Body awareness
(marching tall,
heads high)
Rhythm
through
counting to 4
Awareness of
other children as
they keep in line

Progression:

(a)

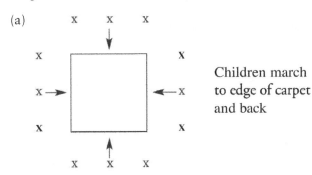

Children march
to edge of carpet
and back

Laterality
(awareness of
sidedness)

All children repeat the pattern they have already learned at the same time, perhaps substituting waving for clapping.

(b) Children on opposite sides go in and out at different times.

Judging size
of step

Jumping
Feet together.

Free jumping, feet together to build consecutive actions.

Jump and jump and wait, jump and jump and wait.
Use arm swing to help propulsion forward.

Progression:

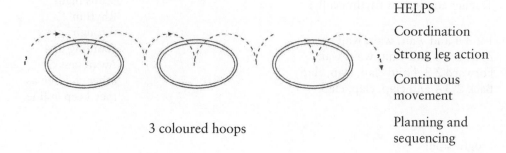

HELPS

Coordination

Strong leg action

Continuous movement

Planning and sequencing

3 coloured hoops

Jump into hoops – 'jump and jump and jump and out'; varying distance.

(Some children will need to 'shuffle' to regain a good preparatory position for the next jump, while others will 'jack-in-the-box'.)

One child per large hoop

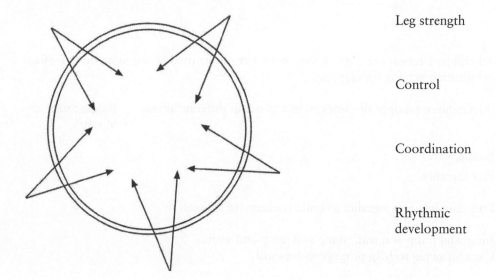

Leg strength

Control

Coordination

Rhythmic development

Jumping in and out in all directions.

Teacher can accompany with tambourine. 1 and 2 and 3 and 4 (jumps).

Rest, get ready – now you're off. 1 and 2 and 3 and 4 and stand quite still and tall.

Balancing

Walking along broad side of bench – head high, looking forward.

Progression 1:

Hold hoop above head as you walk. Keep hoop steady!

Progression 2:

Walking along narrow ledge of bench, with light handhold where necessary. Then alone – trying to feel for position of next step rather than looking down.

Progression 3:

HELPS

Balance
Coordination
Timing
Partner
cooperation

Good poise
Body awareness
Leg strengthening

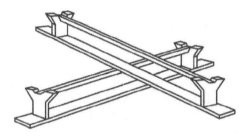

See-saw – two benches sit astride as see-saw
Teacher supervision required.

Progression 4:

Balance
Segmented
movement
Body awareness

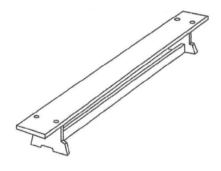

Single bench broad side up.
One foot flat on broad side of bench. Push head high, come down to floor, push high, repeat.

Keep the same foot on the bench till the end.
Repeat using other foot on bench.

Progression 5:

Use the same activity but the narrow side of the bench.   Coordination
Offer some light support so that the child feels the extension.
Emphasise strong straight back and legs.

Progression 6:

Using either the broad or narrow side of the bench as
appropriate – stand well, balance on one foot, arms outstretched.

Draw as large a circle as possible with the other foot (allow time
between turns to correct any overbalancing).
Change over so that circling foot becomes balancing foot.

Bunny jumps.

(1) Freely on floor, emphasising weight evenly balanced on   Transfer of weight
     two hands looking forward and up.   from feet on to
                                                                strong arms.

(2) Over tape/rope or through hoop (trying not to touch   Weight-bearing
     hoop).   strengthening
                                                                for arms/hands.

Progression for most agile children:

Child A holds hoop just above floor level.
Child B bunny jumps through, Child A moving hoop to clear feet.

Using action words

Running (tambourine; shake and shake and shake and HOLD).

Running in limited space, avoiding others – FREEZE,   Negotiating

CRUMPLE down to the floor and SPRING up – (POP)   Listening for
                                                                commands

and RUN.

Progression:	Rhythmical awareness
Half the class stands still (making statues) while others weave in and out – after freeze all the children crumple, then spring up (POP). Change over. Partner runs. Emphasise direction, e.g. run forward, crumple down, spring up.	Partner awareness
(Leave enough time for children to cope. Use the action words, freeze, crumple, pop.)	Directionality

For other ideas, see Appendix 3.

2. Fine motor skills

Equipment	Activity	Helps
1. Sand tray (a) Wet sand	Building castles, sand pies Pulling fingers through to make	Coordination (two hands) Finger awareness Strengthening and dexterity (continuous pathways)
(b) Dry sand	Pouring and filling Patting	Two-handed coordination Aiming: judging quantity Crossing the midline Hand dominance
2. Water tray + tubes and funnels + cake colours + ice + sponge	Pouring and filling Syphoning Mixing Squeezing	Holding implements at different heights for a longer time; spatial awareness Finger strengthening and dexterity
3. Clay	Moulding	Finger and arm strengthening

4. Scissors (+LH scissors) Paper (80–90 gsm) Stiff paper ⟶ light cardboard	Snipping fringes (rugs for doll's house or doilies for snack) then cutting between two straight lines, then easy curved patterns	Manipulation, finger dexterity: timing Two-handed coordination Hand–eye coordination
5. Beads – different colours All sizes – large and smaller holes Stiff string or tightly rolled paper cut in different sizes – previously painted by child	Threading – selecting sizes, colours, patterns	Two-handed and hand–eye coordination Sequencing (colours, sizes of beads) Completing a two-part task
6. Parachute	Billowing the parachute – one child running underneath to other side	Wrist strengthening Timing action in a non-competitive group
7. Lego Large bricks	Construction	Hand dominance Two-handed coordination Sorting and selecting Matching, balancing Crossing the midline
8. Table, cups, plastic knives etc.	Setting the table	Sorting, matching, one-to-one correlation
9. Shapes of coloured card. Small shapes held up by teacher, children run and stand on or by the matching shape on the ground	Teacher and small group in good space	Shape and colour recognition, tracking Problem-solving
10. Hammer, wood, nails	Hammering	Two-handed/eye coordination Dexterity (pincer grip)

11. Dressing-up clothes – shoes and tutus, firemen's helmets, wedding dresses, kilts	Dressing and undressing	Dressing skills Ordering
12. Telephone with dial	Dialling	Finger dexterity Two-handed coordination Turn-taking
13. Computer	Keyboard skills Recognition of shapes, patterns	Tracking from screen to keyboard (vertical to horizontal) helping later copying from board Finger dexterity
14. Empty boxes	Imaginative play	Creative skills, partner play
15. Corners House, hospital, theatre, shop		Role-play activities of daily living Coping skills
16. Flour, water, margarine Baking, mixing, cutting, shaping, rolling dough	Teacher and small group	Two-handed coordination Pincer grip skills Hand strengthening
17. Finger puppets	In twos	Turn-taking Finger dexterity Role play

3. Small games

Game	Organisation	Helps
Simon says 'do this, do that'	Teacher and small group of children	Watching and copying Body awareness Response time Listening
Angels in the snow	Teacher and small group of children	Tactile awareness Spatial awareness
'Head, shoulders, knees and toes' 'Incy wincy spider' and other singing games with actions	Teacher and small group of children	Body awareness Speed of movement Copying
'In and out the dusty bluebells'	Circle of children	Spatial awareness (under, through, round)
Party games e.g. musical beanbags (instead of chairs)	Teacher and small group of children	Listening and responding Speed of movement
Drama, acting out well-known stories, e.g. Jack chopping down the bean-stalk	Teacher and small group of children	Listening Swinging arms Rhythm development

Chapter 6

A positive reflection on observation and assessment

Part 1: initial observations

Just in case there was a presumption that all staff would, without prompting, observe the same things, members of the team were asked: 'What do you see when you meet children for the first time?' This was to find if there was a common basis for assessment, or if there had to be a debate to find common ground with some having to make adjustments and relinquish their preferences. Would this affect joint assessments and forward plans? Or perhaps initial observations would change in the first weeks?

Key questions to clarify observations:

a) What sorts of things do different members of the team observe when they meet their pupils for the first time and to what extent do, or can these guide their planning of learning activities?
b) What are the competences that should feature on an assessment format?

The team was anxious to explain that 'first impressions' were just that, but they considered it was interesting to see if different members of the team had different perspectives and priorities and if these reflected their particular teaching role.

Sophie, a principal teacher, concerned with both management and teaching explained:

> First of all I note whether the children are willing to come into school or whether they are reluctant to do so. This could show whether they are anxious or placid; they might even come over as over confident or aggressive. I always speak directly to the child saying how pleased we are to welcome them into school and see if I get any response. All the staff try to convey to both the children and the parents that they are smiling and caring while being professionally confident too and that they have plans and expectations that each child will progress in the setting.

She did add that children who were autistic were probably unaware of these overtures but that it was important to set the scene, as it were.

> Then I see how the children are with their parents – are they clingy and upset or ready to come to school? I think the child's relationship with the parents is very

important. I look to see if the parents support their child, staying calm and not pushing the child forward or conveying any kind of unease. Often the parents begin by telling us about their child's likes and dislikes and that can guide our approach. Most are anxious to see the classroom and get some idea of the learning that is planned.

So Sophie's first observations were primarily social interaction ones – to see how the children had built relationships with their parents and to find how willing the children were to come into class. She explained that social observations could indicate whether the children would sit happily near another child and be willing to wait till the other children came in to the room. She explained that she could work out seating arrangements from first observations and decide whether the first pieces of interaction/storytelling needed to be calming or lively ones. She had the experience to judge her pacing and timing from first encounters.

Jay, another teacher, looked to see if the children understood instructions and how they responded to others in class. She explained:

> I particularly notice if the children make any overtures to the others and if they show any interest in the resources set out to welcome them. I watch to see if they acknowledge the staff in any way or if they look away or up to the ceiling. I hope they are not going to be too anxious but if they are, we have interesting toys to settle them and calm them down. We have soft music playing and of course the parents are welcome too in the first days. I need to discover whether the children have speech and if their words are clearly articulated or simply sounds. I know that many children can understand much more than they can say and that some can speak at length without understanding what they are talking about, but initially just finding whether they understand me and if they can reply either verbally or through gestures is really important. I also need to check whether the parents know about PECS and signing and if they have preferences or leave it to us to decide what's best.

She aimed to use PECS as a key means of communication especially for those without spoken words. Some parents are wary of PECS, wondering if using symbols would delay their children's acquisition of speech but Jay explained that she always used clear words alongside the pictures or symbols. In this way the pictures encouraged speech. She believed that the system gave the children independence because they could communicate and express their preferences and later come to recognise that they could build symbols into sentences. The team could quickly find what the children wanted just as if speech was present. Turn taking, an important precursor to language was also established. In her classroom a large visual timetable was used to order the events in the day and Jay hoped this would enable the children to understand 'now' and 'next'.

Strategy

In the first few days, Jay organised head and shoulders pictures of the children. These were placed on a velcro strip and the children took their picture off the strip and put it on their plate on a table set for snack. Later, in the same kind of activity, each child was asked to take someone else's picture off the strip and give it to the pictured child. This was to develop communication and help the children recognise each other and learn each other's names.

In contrast Kate, a teacher of physical education, concentrated on the children's motor skills.

> First of all I look at the children walking as they are shown round the school and the playground. I check whether they are balanced and controlled or if they stumble or walk on their toes. I look at their muscle tone and if it's poor I ask the parents if they have splints or walking frames and what physiotherapy they have. This immediately tells me to plan to include extra strengthening activities such as controlled, careful walking or for the more adventurous and able, jumping over low ropes in the gym, or in the playground I'd make sure they could try the small trampoline for bouncing. It's set in the ground so it's completely safe. We don't have a swimming pool here but some time later, once I get to know the parents I'd explain that even walking through deep water is strengthening, developing all the muscles in the legs and trunk because the water provides resistance and I hope that they would take the child there.
>
> Then I watch the children in the outdoor area and see if they will run around or try to balance on the benches and I can see if they can control their bodies. I look to see if they notice the other children and copy what they are doing, if they have ideas of their own or whether they are overwhelmed by being given freedom to choose their activity for a short time. I believe that the motor area is the most revealing – I think there is a strong link with all other aspects of development. If the children are reluctant to move around that can point to a lack of confidence or perhaps they haven't had the opportunity to play outside in a park where there would be apparatus. Often children need time to try things out – just to get used to the environment and each other, because playing with others could be a new experience.
>
> Knowing if, and how, they move lets me think about the first lesson in the gym – whether or not to use music or equipment, how many children should be there at once, what size of space will be best, that kind of thing. First observations can be very revealing, giving up hints as to the best way forward.

Kate explained that a large space could be daunting for some children and that equipment such as balls could cause problems till she had time to establish discipline and trust. She also kept the bikes locked up till she could be sure there would be no accident.

Jake, a nursery nurse who was particularly interested in nutrition, had rather a different view.

> Well I look to see if they show any interest in what's available at snack time. Unfortunately some children don't want to eat anything at all and I make one of my aims to try to make their food appetising. We try small portions and make the plate attractive and they learn to sit at table and eat together. Some children eat well but often crisps or rice cakes are the things they prefer. Recently an article in

the *Telegraph* (October 2014) claimed that broccoli, cauliflower and cabbage could ameliorate the effects of autism. Unfortunately they didn't explain how we would get the children to taste them. The school provides a warm meal followed by yoghurt or jelly as well as apples and bananas and crackers so the children are given a good diet with choices.

I also try to find out if any children have dietary difficulties so that I can alert the kitchen. We have to take the parents' advice as to what they are allowed to eat and we make a careful note of allergies – so many children have a gluten free diet or can't take dairy. It's a big responsibility for us because they can grab something they are not supposed to have. Sometimes the parents know their child won't eat and bring in some food from home. So perhaps I am looking for different things from the others. It's really interesting when we share findings and make new discoveries.

Jake also stressed coping skills:

I think the children should learn to get dressed by themselves because this lets them become more independent and also it can be a help for busy parents. In the same way, eating and drinking at the table is important because then the children learn social skills. I also think that waiting till all the children have finished really helps communication because they have to watch each other and be patient.

I also wonder if they are toilet trained – that's part of my job although everyone deals with toileting and accidents. We have a toilet symbol on our visual timetable but some of the children don't make the connection or they simply don't have the muscle control they require. Some children are still in nappies and that takes a different kind of organisation to make sure we have enough of everything they need to feel fresh and comfortable.

We have a lot of hand washing and teeth cleaning. I also need to plan the resources for that. developing these skills are really part of our curriculum and whenever possible we encourage them to be independent and this takes a great deal of time and patience.

Do these differences in early perception matter? Do the differences facilitate building a comprehensive profile of the child's needs? The answer to this must be 'yes' but to do this there needs to be time for staff to share and appreciate all the recordings. The headteacher Anne answered this 'differences' question:

I think it's a strength if the different members of staff get time to discuss their observations and pull together a profile rather than having just one of the team responsible for an individual child. Individual members of the team have particular interests and skills just as the children do so it's best to let them focus on their areas of expertise. This gives confidence and motivation. Every observation they record makes a contribution to forward planning and meeting the proscribed targets.

These early observations are superseded by more formal dated assessments that monitor progress or regression over time.

These differences, however, gave pause for thought and the team aimed to clarify what they were, by using the four domains of development to provide a structure.

Part 2

The aim was to design an assessment format that would support each child; one that would record progress and be a positive reflection of the way the school was respecting and valuing the pupils. The recordings would also be studied to highlight the most appropriate strategies for taking learning forward. With this in mind, it was decided to begin the process by nominating four general pointers that delineated the basic outcomes of what the school hoped to achieve. These were:

- To give the children a happy time in school
- To boost the children's self-esteem
- To foster social learning and language through play
- To build a repertoire of taught skills where appropriate to help the children cope with the activities of daily living.

And they wished for their assessment policy to reflect these aims.

While these were fairly straightforward to write down, they each covered a whole spectrum of developments that had to be individualised for each child. The team would have to discover what made the children happy i.e. what each preferred to do and build the opportunity for that into the curriculum, preferably through a play event where the team were following the children's lead. Then they could monitor any increase in confidence and competence and if appropriate, teach a specific skill that had arisen through playing.

Boosting the children's self-esteem is of paramount importance but it is very difficult to assess and record any improvement except through competences such as 'being more confident' or 'more willing to participate' or 'appears happier' and to some extent these depend on the perception of the assessor. This is why it is important to share observations amongst staff and, in discussing instances of where the positive change occurred, gather 'evidence' to back up any recording.

The next preparatory stage was to discuss key aspects of the children's development so that one or more could function as the basis of assessment. The number and kind could be changed/expanded as necessary. These were set out as tables that covered the four aspects of or domains of development. While it is slightly artificial to sub-divide competences like this (e.g. should 'learning to sign' be primarily a motor, intellectual, social or emotional competence?), the table does ensure that a balanced assessment covering each child's 'best areas' is at hand. Also, staff discussions about where each competence should be placed can clarify issues and ensure everyone has a say in what is to be assessed. The team then considered a curriculum based on the development of play and built a table of play competences.

From these charts, particular competences can be selected as appropriate for the age and developmental stage of the children.

Table 6.1 Table of competences for assessment for children with ASCs

Intellectual challenges	Movement challenges
Being able to Make a plan: make appropriate, independent choices.	*Being able to* Show increase in competence in carrying out activities of daily living, e.g. make a sandwich.
Increase literacy and mathematical skills.	Put coats on and off; fasten velcro/zips/buttons.
Plan and sequence, e.g. ordering the events in a story.	Control equipment, e.g. catch and throw a balloon or ball safely.
Understand and follow the routine of the day.	Open and close doors with control.
Organise self and resources.	Take part in making/drawing.
Cope with changes in routine.	Get undressed – know the order of setting out clothes.
Recognise and look after own belongings.	Move around without knocking into others; judge personal space of self and others.
Remember favourite songs and recognise what they mean, e.g. 'let's go back to circle'.	Crawl using the cross lateral pattern Sign to communicate.
Use PECS symbols to: a) communicate wishes b) ask for help c) make a sentence, e.g. 'I want a cracker' or 'I want the iPad!' Use signing as appropriate.	Balance, so that basic activities are controlled. Cross the midline of the body. Use both sides of the body in a coordinated way.

Social challenges	Emotional challenges
Being able to Respond to a question or an instruction. Be aware of others.	*Being able to* Accept praise and show pleasure.
Read non-verbal communication, i.e. understand simple gestures. Hold eye contact briefly.	Concentrate and focus; be able to stay with a task, gaining confidence and pleasure from it.
Point to what is wanted. Understand object permanence.	Cope when thwarted; recognise safety boundaries.
Understand that others need attention too.	Be confident in different environments.
Join in with others.	Keep calm, not over-react.
Share resources.	Recognise when someone is angry/hurt/pleased. Applaud others.
Take the initiative; follow a plan.	Show empathy.

Table 6.2 Table of competences to monitor development in play

Intellectual	Movement (motor)
Being able to: Understand what other children are doing. Understand their view may be different.	Being able to: Enjoy large apparatus, e.g. benches and floor trampolines.
Use advanced pretend to appreciate other's feelings, e.g. feeding teddy, knowing he is hungry.	Combine basic movement patterns, e.g. run and jump safely.
	Use the pincer grip to draw.
Use simple pretence, e.g. to feed a doll or put a can into a garage made of bricks.	Cook in the outdoor mud kitchen using utensils appropriately.
	Get dressed in role play costumes.
Play alongside another child (parallel play).	Roll a ball; rebound a ball off a bench and catch it.
Play alone with focus on the activity (solitary, functional play).	Walk securely, changing directions without stumbling.
Recognise that objects out of sight are still there.	Sit well balanced; move to play with control.
Keep immersed in play for a short time.	Crawl (using the cross lateral pattern) over and under obstacles.
Be able to choose something to play with.	Lift, carry and place toys confidently.

Social	Emotional
Being able to: Gain satisfaction from lining up objects.	Being able to: Participate.
Give play items a purpose. Use a 'tool' to make something happen.	Understand and enjoy the play.
Share ideas with another child/adult.	Appreciate the purpose of a play character, e.g. that a doll needs care.
Take turns in a game, e.g. peek-a-boo; round and round the garden.	Handle play resources carefully – recognising their use.
Copy an activity. Be willing to show.	Listen and wait for a turn.
Have pleasure in play and gain self-confidence.	Control anger and aggression.
Play alone, focussing on the activity.	Welcome another player.
Sustain play while being aware of another player (parallel play).	Join another player, e.g. cooperating in building a sand castle.
Play near another child – watch and copy.	Recognise and be pleased at working together.
Cooperate in playing with a friend.	Make a friend through play.

Assessment formats for the youngest children

Callum (Chapter 1) was happy when he was given a piece of banana and his nursery nurse Ellie was building on this to have him use PECS symbols to ask for this treat. He was initiating communication to have his needs met. So the logical, next development would be to have him ask more people for more things!

Callum was silent for most of the day but he regularly indicated by using his PECS book that he wished to go to the sensory room. There, he clearly asked for 'bubbles on'. When highly motivated, he could say these words. Would it be realistic to hope that he might offer more words, perhaps 'blue' to describe the colour of the bubbles? Or perhaps he could work the switch to control the display himself and recognise he was in charge? This would surely boost his self-esteem – although we could only gauge this by any change in expression, his body language and his willingness to try the new word.

See below for examples of four assessment sheets.

Child's name and age:	Observation: date 14/9/14	Plan for action	Assessment: evaluation of plan
Callum 4 years 10 months	Can point to what he wants to have; knows Ellie will help him. Callum can say 'bubbles on' in the sensory room.	Have Callum use more PECS symbols, e.g. to ask for his favourite toy or food. Help him switch on the bubbles and say 'blue' as they work.	Yes he is doing this; now prompt him to make choices. Intrigued by switch and understood cause and effect. Listened to 'blue' but didn't try to say it today.

Thinking now of Jacob (also from Chapter 1) who was reviewing a play episode on his iPad where he and other children in his class were playing outside on the 'bus.' His teacher Ria wondered; a) if he would recognise himself and the other children he knew by name and b) whether this would encourage him to speak.

Child's name and age:	Observation: date 5/1/15	Plan for action	Assessment: evaluation of plan
Jacob 5 years 6 months	Jacob appeared to recognise himself and replayed the episode several times. With prompting, he offered, 'Bus stop'.	As he showed interest in tickets for passengers, he could distribute them and say, 'One, two' as he did so. As yet he does not speak but he is interested in the activity.	The ticket plan encouraged other children to approach the bus and Jacob gradually learned to give one to each child. This develops one-to-one correspondence.

Mia is sustaining play activities for a longer spell since she was praised for feeding the teddy as part of the 'Goldilocks' story. The plan was for the team to introduce other activity stories and see if they could discern her level of pretence.

Child's name and age:	Observation: date 15/12/14	Plan for action	Assessment: evaluation of plan
Mia 5 years 4 months	Mia is fascinated by the large teddy bear and tries to feed him. 'When teddy is very greedy, he get a sore tummy'. Mia nodded. Would this encourage her to say, 'Sore tummy?'	Try to find if Mia understands Teddy's ailment, comforting him by rubbing his tummy. If so she has shown advanced pretend.	Develop this idea using another story with activities, e.g. The Three Little Pigs allows 'huffing' and 'puffing' and also building the houses. Will Mia recognise that the pig who loses his house is sad?

Kieran must be more aware of others and appreciate the effects of his strength on them. He is the biggest boy in the class, full of energy and 'go'. He must learn to moderate his strength in interacting with other children.

Child's name and age:	Observation: date 12/12/14	Plan for action	Assessment: evaluation of plan
Kieran 5 years 1 month	Kieran sometimes doesn't know his own strength – he can push children over.	Help Kieran work with 'soft hands' and 'hard hands' to recognise the difference. Use firm therapy or rolling and coiling snakes. Use the poem 'gently, gently stroke fluffy kitten' from *Jingle Time*.	Need to bring in more examples, e.g. hard hands to use the heavy shovel, soft hands to pick up grapes at snack time. Build transfer opportunities.

Time sampling methods of recording observations

Sometimes observers are unsure of or disagree about what should be the key focus for their observations. This can be clarified by using time sampling, i.e. recording exactly what the child does or doesn't do over short spells. In this way suspicions of difficulties can be confirmed or jettisoned. Either way there is proof to back up further action. In the following example, Ian's teacher was suspicious that he needed strengthening work for poor leg strength. Ian had disguised this by avoiding what he couldn't do well. Other members of the team were unsure that this was the case, so a pie chart was used to confirm Ian's needs.

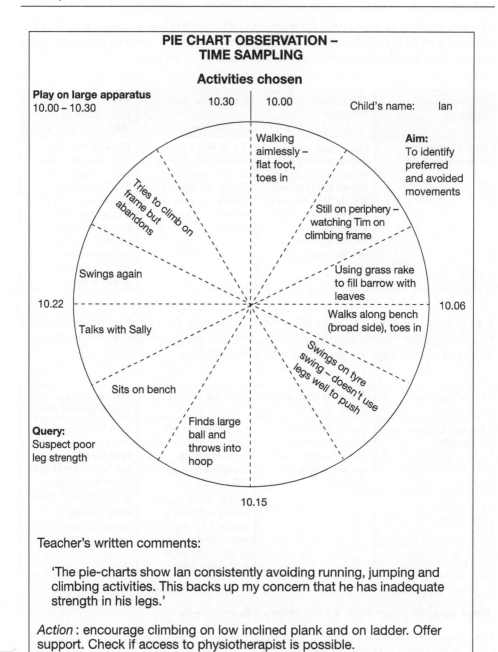

PIE CHART OBSERVATION – TIME SAMPLING

Activities chosen

Play on large apparatus 10.00 – 10.30

Child's name: Ian

Aim: To identify preferred and avoided movements

10.30   10.00

- Walking aimlessly – flat foot, toes in
- Still on periphery – watching Tim on climbing frame
- Using grass rake to fill barrow with leaves
- Walks along bench (broad side), toes in
- Swings on tyre swing – doesn't use legs well to push
- Finds large ball and throws into hoop
- Sits on bench
- Talks with Sally
- Swings again
- Tries to climb on frame but abandons

10.22 .... 10.06

10.15

Query: Suspect poor leg strength

Teacher's written comments:

'The pie-charts show Ian consistently avoiding running, jumping and climbing activities. This backs up my concern that he has inadequate strength in his legs.'

Action : encourage climbing on low inclined plank and on ladder. Offer support. Check if access to physiotherapist is possible.

Number sampling

Sometimes professionals can be accused of 'seeing what they want to see' or 'recording one item as if was pervasive rather than a one-off occurrence'. This is especially so if the children have made rapid progress. A number sampling chart can be filled in by different observers thus providing concrete evidence.

Table 6.3 Some ideas for shared observations

Initiating interaction	Morning break	11.30–11.45 indoors	Staff comments
Beckons friend to join in			
Closes down play and moves off			
Physically prevents others playing			
Tries to share ideas with friend			

The important thing is to select items that are appropriate for the group or the individual being monitored and to record how often they occurred. In this way unforeseen issues might be highlighted and intervention targeted to resolve them.

Results from all these measures can be used as 'evidence' of any progress or problem and so form the basis of 'evidence'. This method is useful for observing a new child when the most pertinent aspect for observation, assessment and profiling has yet to be decided. Each sector of the chart can have several observations and be analysed or discussed later, giving a focus to staff exchanges.

But if the assessment is concerned with coping strategies then a list of key manoeuvres rather than underlying competences is required. This done, the assessors who record children's difficulties have to reconsider what is causing them. Some suggestions are given but these items can be changed or just a few selected.

Table 6.4 Some baseline observations

Coping skills: base line observations	Yes	Not yet	Sometimes
Settles well in the school environment			
Recognises own name			
Recognises names of staff			
Can speak (five words)			
Is trying to speak			
Can listen to instructions			
Can understand instructions			
Can understand the routine of the day			
Can choose food and drink			
Can self-feed yoghurt and jelly			
Can use a straw			
Can put on coat, shoes and socks			
Coping skills (2)			
Recognises daily songs/tries to join in			
Can sit and listen to a short story			
Can remember characters from a story			

(continued)

Table 6.4 (continued)

Coping skills: base line observations	Yes	Not yet	Sometimes
Can use PECS to communicate			
Can undress without help			
Can put clothes on in correct order			
Can understand visual timetable			
Can cope at table			
Coping skills (3)			
Can accompany younger child to bus			
Can select items in a shop and pay			
Can join in activities in the gym			
Can cope in out-of-school activities			
Recognises numbers up to 5			
Recognises phonics (five)			
Can use cutlery			
Can pack bag and carry it home			
Can carry a message home and bring a reply			
Can make a sandwich			
Can follow a chart showing routines			

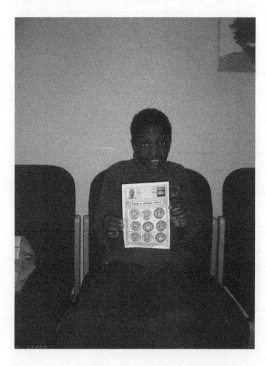

Figure 6.1 Paul shows the pleasure recognition can bring as he shows his completed card. Well done Paul!

Figure 6.2 In this way children see that everyone is aware of the progress they are making.

Observation and assessment is to make things better for the children, to provide evidence of progress for the parents and to show that the dedication and expertise of the school has encouraged the children to be all that they can be, for surely no one can ask for anything more.

The school encourages each child to record their progress on a 'Wall of achievement'. This reinforces their progress; it shows how important this is to everyone who passes and encourages them to walk tall.

The most important and final questions reflect back on the aims of the study, i.e. were the children playing and learning? Were they communicating more and tolerating more change? Were they becoming more skilled in the activities of daily living? Looking at the wall, the answer must be 'YES'.

And perhaps the most important question of all, 'Were the children happy?'

The book finishes with a plea from Gurney (1987).

'Everyone, children and adults, praise yourselves. For sure, no one else could have done it so well.'

Figure 6.3 We have no ruler to measure the smiles but Mia expresses it all.

Final strategies

Here is a summary of strategies that intrigued the children and helped them learn. These were devised through observation, assessment and action and were in addition to the list at the start of the book.

- Use the literature to give guidance but do not allow it to limit what you try to do. As demonstrated by Mia feeding the teddy, children can become involved in pretend play when the literature explained that this was very difficult for children on the spectrum.
- Follow the children's ideas/preferences and develop those. Allow them to learn through play and give them time to formulate words, for motivation can have surprising outcomes. Remember Callum who articulated 'bubbles on' in the sensory room, Mia who asked for 'make-up' for her handbag and Sophia who wanted 'music' when she was in charge of the tape recorder. These were non-verbal children suddenly motivated to speak to have their needs met.
- Have daily practices of skills such as crawling using the cross lateral pattern because of the intellectual gains inherent in the activity. On the cover, see Callum who has mastered the pattern, who is using it to embark on a long crawl through the caterpillar. He has the additional challenge of carrying his bricks so he has quite a balance task ahead! Other crawling/climbing activities, e.g. crawling over piles of cushions, rolled up rugs, through hoops, provide variety and habituate the pattern.
- Transfer learning opportunities from one environment to another and explain the similarity to the children. Remember Jacob who tidied up in the gym and then used his gathering leaves skills in the playground? And Jordan who gave out tickets on the bus? He was learning about one-to-one correspondence in a fun environment. This helped him set the table for snack later on.
- When squabbles arise, e.g. when several children want to drive the bike or bus at the same time, try to use this as an opportunity for them to learn about turn taking and sharing rather than removing the 'bus' from the scene.
- Contextualise learning whenever possible. When the linear PECS symbols were rearranged in a clock face, the children came to know e.g. that 'at three o'clock' it was time to tidy work stations.
- So the time passing and the numerals were learned together. Remember Ryan who compared the PECS clock to his birthday watch?

- Resource the play areas so that transfer of learning can happen. Kieran needed a large rough brush, a shovel and a bin. As he learned about transfer and was praised for his work, he was involved in a strengthening activity.
- Analyse the wider benefits that children get from activities in terms of their social, emotional, motor and intellectual gains. Remember that learning in one sphere is likely to transmit to another in terms of confidence as well as skill. Remember Jill who loved beating the rhythm of a song on the chime bar? She had to listen and wait and prepare as well as handling the equipment. She was in charge – and she loved it!
- Be very aware of children's sensory strengths and difficulties. For those who have never experienced, e.g. constant screening noises (auditory hypersensitivity) it can be difficult to understand how this can defeat any attempts to have the children learn. In similar vein, assess whether retained reflexes are inhibiting the children's development.

  If children have obsessions, e.g. remember Cara who was so overtaken by her party arrangements? Try to find ways to relieve the pressure of having to remember, e.g. cutting out picture of party food and making a collage or scrapbook.
- Above all, praise the children – small steps can lead to wonderful progress, even light bulb moments. And praise yourselves. For sure, no-one else could have worked with the children as well as you do!

Members of staff who played a huge part in supporting this study throughout its development are named below. The children in this school, PROSPECT BANK SCHOOL in Edinburgh, are so fortunate to have such dedicated adults who love them and do everything in their power to enhance their learning and their development. Constantly they are engaging the children in different learning experiences and at Friday assembly the headteacher is in there singing and dancing with the children. I wish learning was like this for all of our children.

Cat Hughes
Grace Smith
Jane Kaczynski
John Ross
Kate Varona, Deputy Head
Kathryn Midwinter
Kirsty Moncrieff
Kirsty Rosie, Headteacher
Lara Russell
Liz Anderson
Nancy Dundas
Sam Palmer
Sandra Ali
Wendy Whyte
Zhara Suliman

Differences in speech and communication across the autistic spectrum

Table A.1

Asperger's syndrome (high-functioning autism?)	Autism	Profound disability
Speech communication Fluent but not flexible ('dictionary speech')	Restricted, pedantic speech. Made-up words – gobbledegook, but important to the child, who repeats and repeats them, often chortling with pleasure	No speech – noises and grunts
No understanding of idiom, sarcasm or jokes	Little comprehension	Silence
Little eye contact	Looks away (peripheral vision may give better focus)	May briefly hold gaze but not comprehend what is intended
May overwhelm others by talking at length about their own interests; they may not stop because they know that someone else's conversation may confuse them	Screams, whirls, cries when frustrated	
Non-verbal communication Cannot interpret non-verbal communication so misinterprets meaning	Bewildered by not understanding – may 'shut down' or 'crash', withdrawing into repeated 'stims'	Little understanding – may respond to careful handling
Intelligence May have high IQ, but more likely to be average	Much lower IQ; early precocity may be memory of others' words rather than own sentences	May smile or be able to indicate unhappiness
'Islets of brilliance' may depend on obsession and eye for detail. No transfer of learning	Omits personal pronouns – 'I'	Sometimes appears to understand but is not able to respond
Prodigious memory for facts and objects; no personal detail offered	Restricted speech, covering own wants	

(continued)

Table A.1 (continued)

Asperger's syndrome (high-functioning autism?)	Autism	Profound disability
Comments correctly but inappropriately; doesn't realise hurt because of not empathising with others	Doesn't say, 'Look at ...' or share interests	
	May have immediate or delayed echolalia (repetition of others' speech, like an echo)	
Understanding By adolescence, will question own differences and may understand and explain condition to others	Doesn't realise own differences, or at least cannot convey the realisation	
May have a sense of guilt	No sense of guilt or duplicity; doesn't bear grudges. No sense of pride	Has emotions but doesn't understand the emotions of others
Movement A strange, stilted gait is common	Little sense of danger seems to protect the children as they climb and swing	Motor milestones very delayed. Probable use of standing frames. All equipment needs to be padded. Easily disorientated by changing directions
Can take part in activities but the children have difficulty in following rules, e.g. changing ends in a game	Trampolining is a favourite with many	

Visual timetables

Some examples of visual timetables.

1) PECS charts with extensions to aid telling the time (an opportunity to transfer learning).

Figure A. I The simple visual timetable shows children what comes next and takes away the stress of having to remember. When an activity is over, the children remove the symbol from the chart. This helps the children appreciate 'now' and 'next'.

The development is in two stages. The first transfers the symbols onto a circle representing a clock face so that the children begin to appreciate time passing in a different way.

The second is a more realistic representation of a clock face with numbers as in a real clock or watch. When the hands point to ten o'clock as one example, the children know it is time for snack and one of them fetches the symbol for snack and attaches it to the clock face. In this example the children have chosen small group story time. This is a new idea – symbols will gradually build up till several are on the chart.

Figure A.2 The last section of the day is set out in pictures.

Figure A.3 The children attach PECS symbols to the clock face to show they appreciate the times when events should happen.

N.B. As there are usually several activities within quarter or half an hour the clock face should be large. If the symbols are left in place then the clock can act as a focus for recall at the end of the day, reminding the children of the different things they have done.

Figure A.4 A visual chart helps children put clothes on in the correct order. Gradually items can be removed or exchanged when the weather changes or when the child remembers without looking. Any chart that helps develop independence is useful.

Figure A.5 Photo sequences are useful reminders of the order of events. To prepare sequences, activities have to be analysed to find the key parts. Reminding children to follow the sequence prevents the child's name always being called out!

The aim is always to reduce stress so that the children find that play and learning is pleasurable – the aim is to have them enjoy the things they want to do.

An introduction to autistic spectrum disorders

It is difficult to adequately describe the difficulties housed in autistic spectrum disorder conditions because no two affected children, even in the same family are alike. Their difficulties are profound and long lasting but all the children can respond to gentle therapies.

Those at the high functioning end of the spectrum can have moderate, even exceptional abilities, often in a narrow field. But they still have the social communication difficulties that are part of the condition. The children with 'pure' autism, however, i.e. those at the lowest end of the spectrum will need care and support for all of their lives. Ongoing research is trying to find a breakthrough and there are instances of children who experience great improvement. But other children, despite many therapies remain locked in a 'silent, terrifying world where nothing intuitively makes sense' (Jane Asher).

If the children are 'high functioning' (previously this would be called Asperger's syndrome), then they can learn how to cope socially, but this takes much time, careful explanations and practice. Parents and teachers need a great deal of patience before the children achieve what others spontaneously do. The children will be intellectually more able; they will certainly have language although this may be stilted and strange. Five per cent may even have a pocket of brilliance (mono savants). They may also have the commitment that develops original creative ideas and makes them hugely successful, e.g. Temple Grandin, a high functioning autist is an author and university professor. She has tremendous focus and commitment. Yet the social communication difficulties, the sensory problems, possibly the obsessive behaviour and an inability to empathise with others (the children lack what Robin Baron-Cohen calls 'a theory of mind') still endure. These are sure to make the children 'different'.

So, what is autism? How many children are affected? Why is there such an increase in the numbers of children affected and what can be done to help them? There are many questions and some have no answers, or perhaps just tentative maybes, but when autism affects so many of our children, we are grateful that so many dedicated people are trying desperately to find ways to break down the barriers to understand these complex conditions.

Autism is a lifelong neurological disorder that affects how children and adults experience their world. The condition is not likely to be apparent at birth, (although later some mums reflect on a strange rigidity in their child), but at four months or so, watchful parents may suspect that something is amiss. This could be due to the child's lack of communicative intent, i.e. in avoiding eye contact, by failing to stretch their arms to be lifted, by simply looking blank or disinterested in what is going on. Researchers have found that many tiny babies only scan the lower half of their mother's faces so from the start, from failing to read eye messages, their social learning is diminished. However, this takes skilled observation especially if the baby has no siblings for comparison and children may be two and a half or so before communication difficulties, e.g. lack of language and bonding, are confirmed and aged four before a formal diagnosis is made by a psychologist or paediatrician.

Having their child placed on the spectrum is hugely distressing for all parents. Their child may have had the baby babble or even one or two words, so appeared totally alright, but at around two and a half this disappears and the child has to painstakingly relearn words and phrases. In severe cases the child may never speak again. Often parents feel that 'inside this different child is our own – the wonderful one that we have lost' (parent of a recently diagnosed child). They pray that their child will emerge from autism and search for the key. The confusing thing is that some therapies appear to help some children and not others and the trial and error path is both disheartening and expensive.

The triad of impairments in autism and Asperger's syndrome are identified by Wing and Gould (1979, pp. 11–29) and used by the World Health Organisation as:

- Social: impaired, deviant and extremely delayed social development especially interpersonal development
- Language and communication: impaired and deviant language and lack of communication both verbal and non-verbal
- Thought and behaviour: rigidity of thought and impoverished imagination. No understanding of yesterday or tomorrow.

And sadly, many affected children have dietary and other health problems too.

Social difficulties

The most common phrase used to describe children with autism is that they will not hold eye contact. When contact is tried, they turn away, signalling rejection and this can be disconcerting and hurtful for those seeking interaction. This is because the children see the complex, constantly changing expressions of others as totally confusing and meaningless. They cannot read the meaning that is conveyed by facial expressions or body language. And as 90 per cent of the meaning in a message is transmitted in this way, their understanding is severely or totally diminished. Teachers try to present visual images of different expressions to try to help the children understand what others are attempting to convey, but in interactions, facial expressions change rapidly, and a smile doesn't always convey liking or warmth.

All children on the spectrum have impaired social development and this prevents them making friends. The children do not relate to others in a personal way. One able autistic child asked 'What is a friend?' replied, 'It is someone who carries your books' and, even when prompted, no personal characteristics were forthcoming. Some children on the spectrum *do* want friends but have no idea how to make friendships happen. Prompted by their parents, some will memorise friendly overtures but when these are said out of context, they can sound very strange and cause other children to go away, leaving them disillusioned and not understanding why their entreaties were rebuffed. Many children with autism will make no social overtures at all and so they become isolated. The children themselves may not appear to notice this lack and prefer to be alone because that is less stressful.

- Language – Some children will have no speech, others will use pedantic speech/ learned phrases that do not fit the situation, while others, may speak 'too much' unaware of the effect this is having on others. Turn taking, listening to others and pausing to ascertain the effect the 'conversation' has on others has to be explained – many times.

Children on the spectrum do not understand idiom or sarcasm (thankfully this kind of interaction is no longer part of education) and everyday phrases are understood literally, e.g. 'Has the cat got your tongue?' can cause real anxiety about their own safety and an aversion to cats or, 'Don't hurry, will you?' can cause a child to delay even more. How confusing it all is! Or when a disaster happens, a perplexed and wearied parent can come out with, 'That's just *great*'. It is not difficult to understand the confusion when the child, not appreciating the intonation, sees this as praise, an indication that the incident should happen again! This strange lack of understanding and the disappearing speech are the first and most common factors that parents share when bringing their children for assessment.

Some children later found to be autistic will have prolific early speech but much of this will be mimicked rather than made up speech. It can be hard to spot the difference till strange utterances are spotted. Charlotte Moore explains that when her son was given a toy telephone, he did not volunteer 'Hello', as most neurotypical children would, but perfectly mimicked a previously heard phrase, 'Please replace the handset and try again later'. Some children will repeat learned phrases that sound alright in context, e.g. asking, 'What kind of car have you got?'. But then the same phrase will be repeated minutes later when the question is no longer relevant. Furthermore, the child is not likely to wait for or be interested in the reply!

When children talk like this, the reactions from others must make them feel very strange. Perhaps 'not understanding' contributes to their reluctance to interact with others? Children often withdraw and lose the speech they had. Perhaps when they reach two and a half, the demands put on them overwhelm them to the extent that they retreat into their own safer world where no demands are made to stress them?

- Thought and behaviour – Adhering to routines; not realising that if adults are not present, they 'can't know' what is going on and so cannot take appropriate steps to stop it happening again.

Children on the spectrum often have a rigid adherence to routine. It is reassuring if unchanging timetables structure their day. If they can build a mental model of what will happen in their day, then they can feel secure, but any deviations can cause real distress, possibly evidenced by screaming, aggression or withdrawal. Taken further, this routine may develop into obsessions, e.g. only walking home by one route, only drinking from a yellow cup, refusing to eat at all. These provide comfort to the child but bewilderment to the parents. They are all different and may last for months and suddenly disappear, and another obsession may take hold. In some children and adults with high functioning autism who find their 'differences' or obsessions are valuable to others, they can lead to high-level careers. This is because of the combination of high ability and workaholic commitment. The aforementioned Dr Temple Grandin is a good example of this. She is a highly respected author and teacher who found that she felt calmer when she was held firm. She also found communicating with animals easier than with people. This led to her designing cattle crushes so that animals could be held still and be calm as they received their medication and she has lectured all over the world on this topic. But if the obsession is collecting used tickets or lollipop sticks and lining them up, then this doesn't happen. However, it is hoped that the children gain comfort from their obsessions and routines and that somehow they are filling a gap in their lives.

Differences like these can cause the children to be bullied and careful observation by teachers is essential because even the children with speech won't tell. Why not? Because they think their parents or teachers already know! They don't realise that if adults are not present, then they can't know! And if children do try to tell, they may well miss the personal part of the story that holds the key to understanding. This makes supporting them very difficult.

Children on the spectrum have a total absence of pretence and while this means they are truthful children without pride or envy, this lack also limits their imaginative play. The children very often lack the imagination to deal with events removed from the here and now. As Jane Asher, president of the National Autistic Society, explains, 'we need imagination to remember yesterday and picture tomorrow'. People need to consider how disabling it is for children not to be able to do these things.

In the early years it is revealing to watch autistic children playing with a toy. They may use it as a comforter or as a 'spam', i.e. something to whirl or flap, but they will not give the toy a personality or build a story around it. Teachers need to be vigilant to spot this difference when there are many other children to be cared for. The 'play' of an autistic child will be qualitatively different. It will be repetitive and depersonalised. Yet careful observation and timely pertinent intervention within a play framework can help develop language and communication.

Assessment must consider both verbal (all autists have difficulties here) and non-verbal intelligence, which can concern activities such as completing jigsaws, understanding puzzles or sorting things into groups.

So there are profound implications for children diagnosed as being on the autistic spectrum and for their families too as understanding and support will be needed throughout the children's lives. And of course children can be more or less affected by the condition.

What causes autism?

Although several and sometimes conflicting theories (e.g. inherited 'faulty' genes vs. brain injury during development vs. too much prenatal testosterone) have been put forward, as yet there is not one agreed cause. The link to the MMR inoculation has been disproved. However, there is no dispute about the claim that the condition is neither caused nor acerbated by poor parenting skills.

The increase in numbers of people being diagnosed is startling – the National Autistic Society claim a 45 per cent increase in the number of autistic children last year giving 2,204 Scottish children in 2004 and of course many more in England due to the higher numbers of children there. It has been mooted that there are 125,000 children affected by autism in the UK. In their study of the prevalence of ASD (autistic spectrum disorders) Keen and Ward (2004) found that in a single, relatively small health district, the number of recorded diagnoses had doubled over a four year period. They explain this by referring to the current recognition of ASD in more able children and the work to identify the co-occurrence of autism within other severe verbal disorders.

The increase in part must be due to better diagnosis and widening sets of criteria, but non-scientific reminiscence must prompt the question, 'Where were they all when I was at school? There were no children flapping and wailing in the corner then' (Charlotte Moore – mother of three sons, two with autism). Before this survey, the usual ratio given was 1:165, it is now 1:100 children and some areas say 1:49! The boys: girls ratio is 5:1 with the ratio 10:1 for high functioning autism. Some families have a clearly inherited form of autism – and in these cases more girls are affected, but it is more usually boys who have the condition.

For many children on the spectrum, the environment is full of distractors that prevent them focusing and learning. For them, bright lights, loud noises and colourful toys can be very distressing. Their senses become overloaded and their coping strategy can be to 'shut down' or to flap their hands in distress, to shout and scream or self-harm. Some parents have to watch their children regress until they are almost unreach-able and even in milder cases the parents have to change their expectations and learn different ways of bringing up their child. This is very hard; however, children on the spectrum are not envious, whining to get something someone else has. Free of any guile, they are often trustworthy and open. They are totally uninterested in the latest craze. They relate best to those who put no pressure on them. This is hard for parents and teachers who are anxious that they learn the social 'rules' that make life easier for neurotypical children, e.g using a knife and fork. Children with autism might ask, 'when fingers are easier – where's the sense in that?'

No one knows exactly what causes autism and there is no cure. However, 'the role played by genetic influences has been clearly established' (Micali *et al.* 2004). They cite the statistics – concordance rates for monozygotic twins pairs as being in the 60–80 per cent range and heritability estimates at more than 90 per cent. The sibling recurrence rate is 5 per cent or 1:20 for autism and 8 per cent for ASD. Often parents can be surprised by being asked questions about family history but very often on close reflection, they identify genetic clues. Perhaps grandpa or even an uncle showed strange traits, which in the light of new findings could be shown to be autistic. Of course in older generations 'differences' were hushed up or denied and children were institutionalised and labelled ineducable. Some parents were even told to 'go home and forget'.

But of course today, the key intention is to support the children in every aspect of their lives. Hence the stimulus for the book that intends to identify and share strategies for ways to support the children.

Other strategies to support the children's learning

1) The TEACCH Programme (parents and schools working together)

Notes from the Internet on the TEACCH programme

The main goal of TEACCH for autistic children is to help them grow up to a maximum autonomy at adult age. This includes helping them understand the world that surrounds them, acquiring communication skills that will enable them to relate to other people and giving them as much as possible the necessary competence to be able to make choices concerning their own lives.

The major thrust is toward improving communication skills and autonomy to the maximum of the child's potential, using education as a means to achieve that goal. Educational programmes are revised frequently, according to the child's maturation and progress. The children are given rewards for achieving small tasks.

Educational strategies are established individually on the basis of a detailed assessment of the autistic persons learning status and abilities, trying to identify potential for acquisition of skills rather than deficits.

The assessment called PEPr, Psycho Educational Profile tries to identify areas where the person 'passes', i.e. knows what items are used for, areas where the skill isn't there yet, and areas where the skill is emerging. These domains are then put in an individual education programme. This assessment is multi-dimensional. This is a must since there is a great variability of skills, even in the same autistic person, from one domain of competency to the other.

As opposed to behaviour modification, these strategies do not work on the behaviour directly but on underlying conditions that will foster learning experiences. They also make use of recent cognitive psychology research results about some differences in particular areas of brain processing in those with autism. The approach calls for efforts to understand the underlying reasons for this behaviour problem: anxiety, physical pain, difficulty with the task, unpredictable changes and/or boredom.

2) The Son-Rise programme

This is an American home-based programme where a parent or carer interacts on an intensive one-to-one basis in a setting specially designed to have few distractions. The key factor is that the carer observes the child closely and tries to build communication through copying what the child does and providing the words to describe the action, e.g. the adult would say 'spin' if the child exhibits a schema of spinning a coin. Once even brief eye contact is gained the procedure is repeated and interactions are extended in the same way. The authors of the programme claim that it will break down the barriers of autism.

3) ABA (Applied Behaviour Analysis)

This involves behaviour modification utilising part of Skinner's stimulus – response theory and an intensive 1–1 method. This combination teaches appropriate behaviours through breaking down activities into very small steps and rewarding correct responses. The method focuses on the development of personal skills. It has to be noted that the rewards should be chosen by the children who may have very different notions as to what they should be. Choices have varied from having an Elastoplast to being allowed to sit on the radiator. The teacher must be able to understand the key to the children's motivation.

4) PECS (Picture Exchange System)

This picture exchange system involves the use of pictures or children's drawings of things that help the children who have little or no speech to communicate their wishes. The children hand over the picture of a cup to show they would like a drink and this simple exchange allows them a measure of independence. The system can gradually become more complex and be used to develop sentences. Some academics claim that it is a subset of ABA – i.e. concentrating on getting results without addressing the root of the problem. Teachers in the main (my findings) have found the system very helpful and this system is described extensively throughout the book.

Both of these methods should be recorded on IEPs. The system is home, community and school based and so success depends on cooperation amongst all who interact with the child. These systems are facilitators and do not claim cures for autism.

Bibliography

Arron, J. (2006) NFAT dysregulation by increased dosages of DSCR11 and DYRKIA on chromosome 21. *Nature* 441: 595–9.

Asher, J. (2002) Autism: the problem is understanding. Video produced by the National Autistic Society. London.

autism.org.uk (2015)

Baron-Cohen, S. (1989) Do autistic children have obsessions and compulsions? *British Journal of Clinical Psychology* 28(3): 193–200.

Baron Cohen, S. (1991) The development of a theory of mind in autism: Deviance and delay. *Psychiatric Clinics of North America* 14: 33–51.

Baron-Cohen, S., Wheelwright, S. and Jolliffe, T. (1997) Is there a 'language of the eyes'? *Visual Cognition* 4(3): 311–31.

Barrett, S., Prior, M. and Manjiviona, J. (2004) Children on the borderlands of autism: differential characteristics in social, imaginative, communicative and repetitive behaviour domains. *Autism: The International Journal of Research and Practice*, 8(1): 61–87.

Barry, T. D., Klinger, L.G., Lee, L.G., Parlady, N., Gilmore, T. and Bodin, S.D. (2003) Examining the effectiveness of a social skills group for high functioning autists. *Journal of Autism and Developmental Disorders* 33: 489–507.

Bee, H. and Boyd, S. (2005) *The Developing Child (International Edition)*. Boston, MA: Pearson Publications.

Bondy, A. (2012) The unusual suspects: myths and misconceptions associated with PECS. *The Psychological Record* 62: 789–816.

Boutot, A., Crozier, S. and Guenther, T. (2005) Play: teaching play skills to young children with autism. *Education and Training in Developmental Disabilities* 40: 285–92.

Carter, R. (2000) *Mapping the Mind*. London: Orion Books.

Casenhiser, D.M., Shanker, S.G. and Stieben, J. (2013) *Learning Through Interaction in Children with Autism*. Sage Publications.

Charman, T. (2003) Why is joint attention a pivotal skill in autism? *Philosophical Transactions B* 358(1430): 798.

Dixon, P. (2005) *Let Me Be: A Cry For the Rights of Creativity and Childhood in Education*. Winchester: Peche Luna Publications.

Flores, M., Musgrove, K., Renner, S. and Hinton, V., Strozier, S. and Franklin, S. (2012) A comparison of communication using the Apple iPad and a picture based system. *Augmentative and Alternate Communication* 28(2): 74–84.

Garfinkle, A.N. and Schwartz, I.S. (2002) Peer imitation: increasing social interactions in children with autism and other developmental disabilities in inclusive preschool classrooms. *Topics in Early Childhood Special Education* 22: 26–38.

Goddard, S. (2002) *Reflexes, Learning and Behaviour*. Eugene, OR: Fern Ridge Press.

Goddard-Blythe S. (2005) *The Well Balanced Child*. Stroud: Hawthorn Press.

Grandin, T. (2014) *The Autistic Brain*. London: Rider Books.

Greenspan S.I. and Wieder S. (1998) *The Child with Special Needs: Encouraging Intellectual and Emotional Growth*. Reading, MA: Addison-Wesley.

Gurney, P. (1987) Self-esteem enhancement in children: a review of research findings. *Educational Research* 29(2).

Harris P.L. and Lipian, M.S. (1989) Understanding Emotion and Experiencing Emotion. In Saarni, C. and Harris P.L. (eds) *Children's Understanding of Emotion*. New York: Cambridge University Press.

Hein, S. (2005) *History and Definition of Emotional Intelligence*. Englewood Cliffs, NJ: Prentice Hall.

Hughes F.P. (1998) Play in Special Populations. In Spodek, B. and Saracho, O. (eds) *Multiple Perspectives on Play in Early Childhood Education* (pp. 71–193). Albany, NY: SUNY Press.

Hughes, P.L. (1989) *Children and Emotion: the Development of Psychological Understanding*. Oxford: Blackwell Publishers.

Ingersoll, B., Dvortesak, A., Whalen, C. and Sikora, D. (2003) The effects of a developmental social pragmatic language intervention on rate of expressive language production in young children with autistic spectrum disorders. *Focus on Autism and Other Developmental Disorders* 20 (4): 213.

Ingersoll, B.R. (2003). Teaching children with autism to imitate using a naturalistic treatment approach: Effects on imitation, language, play, and social behaviors. *Dissertation Abstracts International: Section B: The Sciences and Engineering*, 63, 6120.

Isaacs, S. (1937) *Social Development in Young Children*. London: Routledge.

Jarrold, F.P. (1998), Boucher, J. and Smith, P. (1996) Generativity deficits in pretend play in Autism. *British Journal of Developmental Psychology* 14: 275–300.

Kasari, C., Gulsrud, A.C., Wong, C., Kwon, S. and Locke, J. (2010) Randomised controlled caregiver joint engagement intervention for toddlers with autism. *Journal of Autism and Developmental Disorders* 40(9): 1045–56.

Keen, D. and Ward, S. (2004) *Autistic Spectum Disorders: A Child Population Profile*. London: Sage.

Lam, G.Y. and Yeung S.S. (2012) Cognitive deficits and symbolic play in preschoolers with autism. *Research in Autistic Spectrum Disorders* 6: 560–64.

Lerna, A., Esposito, D., Conson, M. and Massagli, A. (2014) Long-term effects of PECS on social–communicative skills of children with autism spectrum disorders: a follow-up study. *International Journal of Language and Communication Disorders* 49(4): 478–85.

Leslie, A.M. (1987) Pretence and representation: the origins of theory of mind. *Psychological Review*, 94: 412–26.

Lewis, V. (2003) Play and language in children with autism. *Autism: The International Journal of Research and Practice* 7: 391–9.

McConnell, S.R. (2002) Interventions to facilitate social interaction for young children with autism. *Journal of Autism and Developmental Disorders* 32: 351–73.

Macintyre, C. (2003) *Jingle Time*. Abingdon: David Fulton Publishers.

Macintyre C. (2010) *Play for Children with Special Needs* (2nd edition). Abingdon: Routledge.

Macintyre, C. (2012) *Enhancing Learning Through Play* (2nd edition). Abingdon: Routledge.

Mastrangelo, S. (2005) An analysis of children's social interaction for children with autism: Process and outcomes of a peer mediated buddy program. *Good Autism Practice* 6: 38–50.

Mastrangelo, S. (2009a) Play and the child with autistic spectrum disorders. *International Journal of Play Therapy* 18(1): 13–30.

Mastrangelo, S. (2009b) Harnessing the power of play – Opportunities for children with Autistic Spectrum Disorders. *Teaching Exceptional Children*, 42: 34–44.

Mechling, L.C. (2007) Assistive technology as a self-management tool for prompting students with intellectual disabilities to initiate and complete daily tasks: A literature review. *Education and Training in Developmental Disabilities*, 41: 870–8.

Micali, N., Chakrabarti, S. and Fombonne, E. (2004) The broad autism phenotype: findings from an epidemiological study. *Autism* 8(1): 21–37.

Moore, C. (2012) *George and Sam*. London: Viking.

Murdock L.C., Ganz, J. and Crittendon J. (2013) Use of an iPad Play Story to increase play dialogue of preschoolers with ASD. *Journal of Autism, Developmental Discord* 43: 2174–89.

National Autistic Society (NAS) (2015)

Nithianantharajah, J. and Hannan, A. J. (2006) Enriched environments, experience-dependent plasticity and disorders of the nervous system. *Nature Reviews Neuroscience*, 7: 697–709.

Orr, R. (2003) *My Right to Play: A Child with Complex Needs*. Philadelphia PA: Oxford University Press.

Paley, V. (2005) *A Child's Work: the Importance of Fantasy Play*. Chicago, IL: The University of Chicago Press.

Peer, L. (2004) *Otitis media: a new dimension in Dyslexia*. Paper presented at the BDA International Conference. University of Warwick.

Prelock, P.A. (2006) *Autistic Spectrum Disorders: Issues in Assessment and Intervention*. Baltimore, MD: Paul Brookes.

Prizant, B.M., Wetherby, A.M. and Rydell P.J. (2000) Communication intervention: issues for young children with autism spectrum disorders. In A.M. Wetherby and B.M. Prizant (eds) *Autism Spectrum Disorders – a Transactional Developmental Perspective* (pp. 193–224). Baltimore, MD: Paul Brookes.

Ricamato, M. (2008) The power of sign language helps children with autism create meaning in language. Available online at: www.Signingtime.com (Article in Signing for children with autism).

Rizzolatti, G. and Fabri-Destro, M. (2009) Mirror neurons: From discovery to autism. *Experimental Brain Research* 200 (3–4): 223–37.

Rutherford, M.S., Young, G.S., Hepburn, S. and Rogers, S. (2007) A longitudinal study of pretend play in autism. *Journal of Autism and Developmental Disorders* 37: 1024–10.

Stromer, R., Kimball, J.W., Kinney, E.M. and Taylor, B.A. (2006) Activity schedules, computer technology and teaching children with autistic spectrum disorders. *Focus on Autism and Other Developmental Disabilities* 21: 14–24.

Sutton-Smith, B. (1997) *The Ambiguity of Play*. Cambridge, MA: Harvard University Press.

Terpstra J.K., Higgins K. and Pierce, T. (2002) Can I play? Classroom based interventions for teaching play skills to children with autism. *Focus on Autism and Other Developmental Disabilities*. 17(2): 119–27.

Toth, K., Munson, J., Meltzoff, A.N. and Dawson, G. (2006) Early predictors of language development in young children with ASD: joint attention, imitation and toy play. *Journal of Autism and other Developmental Disorders*, 36: 993–1005.

van Praag, H., Kempermann, G. and Gage, F. H. (2000) Neural consequences of environmental enrichment. *Nature Reviews Neuroscience*, 1: 191–8.

Wan, C.Y. (2011) Auditory-motor mapping, training as an intervention to facilitate speech output in non-verbal children with autism. A proof of concept study. PLoS One 6, No9, e25505.

Wieder, S. and Greenspan, S.I. (2003) *Engaging Autism: the Floor Time Approach to Helping Children Relate, Communicate and Think*. Pittsburgh, PA: Perseus Books.

Williams White, S., Koenig K. and Scahill L. (2006) Social skills development in children with Autism Spectrum Disorders: a review of intervention research. *Journal of Autism and Developmental Discord* 37: 1858–68.

Wing, L. and Gould, J. (1979) The definition and prevalence of autism: a review. Elliot House, Kent: The Centre for Social and Communication Disorders.

Winston, R. (2004) *The Human Mind*. London: Bantam Books

Wolfberg, P.J. (1999) *Play and Imagination in Children with Autism*. New York. Teachers College Press.

Wolfberg, P.J. (2003) *Peer Play and the Autistic Spectrum: The Art of Guiding Children's Socialisation and Imagination*. Shawnee Mission, KS: Autism Asperger Publishing Company.

Woo, C.C. and Leon, M. (2013) Environmental enrichment as an effective treatment for autism: A randomized controlled trial. *Behavioral Neuroscience* 127(4): 487–97.

Index